murmurs at the gate

by

Suzanne S. Rancourt

murmurs at the gate

by

Suzanne S. Rancourt

Brought to the trade by Ingram. Ebooks distributed through Smashwords.

Attention schools and businesses: for discounted copies on large orders,
please contact the publisher directly.

For information contact:
Unsolicited Press
Portland, Oregon
www.unsolicitedpress.com
orders@unsolicitedpress.com
619-354-8005

Cover Design: Kathryn Gerhardt
Cover Photo: Tif Holmes
Editor: Jay Kristensen Jr.

ISBN: 978-1-947021-92-1

Table of Contents

III

To all my Brothers and Sisters who sacrifice their innocence for the good of others.

I simply want to express my profound gratitude to all the friends, family, and community members who have supported my writing and the completion of murmurs at the gate. A sincere thank you goes out to all the readers and editors of this expansive collection of work in its various working titles, and renditions. Your honest feedback, your integrity as fellow artists has brought murmurs at the gate to this place of voiced poetry: Strength and courage, strength and beauty.

I

The Viewing

I want to write about you
because you are still here.
You were never a tall person. Your height
reflected the size of woodland People.
rounder now
but not in the photo as a young man pressing your back
into the Desoto's closed trunk and the heel
of your boot hooked onto the curved, chrome bumper,
hands stuffed in slash pockets of your leather jacket—
Appalachian James Dean.

As a child I noticed your hands—
thick as Oak roots, wide as Bear paws—
were like your father's. I noticed
when you handled a wrench, gripped the truck's steering wheel,
or when you removed that petrified baby rabbit
from the middle of the logging road. Both of you
rounded, brown and small, crouched
before the rolling dust and grill of a chugging Detroit Diesel.

Hoisting with your Popeye arms
you swung yourself into the truck cab.
Your feet barely reached the clutch, brakes, and accelerator.
I asked, "Why did you do that?"
releasing emergency brakes with your 29" inseam leg
and slight grinding of gears, you said, "It ain't easy bein' small."

I didn't think of you as being small.
Your gestures were always big
like the day you said, "C'mon, Suzy, Herbert's killed the bears."
You pulled your height upright,
charged across the lawn and headed next door.
You took the shortcut
through the spruce trees, down the banking to the road
that only us kids and dogs used.
I skip-trotted to keep up.
My calloused feet and stubbed toes
kicked up patty-puffs of roadside sand.

Herbert lived next door. Already a crowd had congregated
to view bodies displayed side by side belly down
noses parallel. When Herbert talked
he sucked his teeth, the sound, almost
as sharp as snapping gum, he'd squint his eye opposite
the corner of the mouth that leered
when he sucked his teeth. As though
flesh was stuck between them.

"C'mon, Suzy, Herbert's killed the bears"
and we went to see our relations
rendered waste by bad blood and heat. To see for ourselves
our family—a boar, a sow, and two cubs—the adults, largest in the state.
All lived behind our house on the mountain.
You showed me their tracks.
How they marked trees, rolled logs, where they fished.

When they mated in the hollow, they screamed like women.
You said they were harmless.
They had their space and we had ours.

Herbert killed the bears, sucked his teeth
and told how easy it was to kill babies,
how the male required more—
heavier trap, shorter chain, more bullets—
Herbert just killed.

You spit a puckering spit that shook the Earth
when it hit just inches from Herbert's feet.
"C'mon, Suzy, we've seen enough."

When the Wind Stops

We were not allowed to stay with our family or community
where we fed our animals and grew our gardens, foraged
for wild food and medicines. Most of the harder changes
had come and gone. I only remember some of the old ways.
Papa doesn't sing anymore.
He sleeps a lot—we don't get to bathe like before
like when we would light candles around the tree—
stars of life—painted the ox horns red and black.

The desert sand could be molded to fit our bones for comfort.
The sidewalk tile is painted and unyielding. It doesn't hurt me much
it hurts Papa. He sleeps a lot. We don't eat much. Papa's bones
have become angled with the new life of no life,
filthy feet, lice and soiled clothing. We have one cup, enamel,
it holds our sustenance—coins, grains of rice, sometimes tea.
Sometimes I pretend that I recognize people from our family,
our clan of wanderers, healers, singers—I run up to them
holding my cup, grabbing their hand as children do.
The men sometimes touch with the pads of their fingers around my lips
put gold in my cup and say they will buy me when I am older.

Papa cries to sleep. "We are hostages" he says, "to progress, engineers,
strangers with no color pressing black boxes to their faces paying gold
for our moments of no moments." Papa sleeps on a pillow
stuffed with grime. The no-color-skin man touches my mouth and says
"You should never grow old" and presses the corner of my curved lip
with the same finger that presses the shiny button on the black box.

I am frightened and not frightened.
I remember sleeping in oxcarts in cool desert nights with stars

our home was larger than all the palaces
we spun like turrets—arms up as pinnacles
in dresses and wraps of glitter and woven reds
brass and ivory arm bangles clacked and rung rhythmically
to the clay drums, click sticks, and gut–string.

I swirl loose tea in my chipped cup
like desert wind far away from sitting
in the sharp square of Papa's sleeping hip, corner of
clay wall, painted tile floor—the backs of my legs are cool
getting longer. I am growing up
and the men will one day buy me because I could not stop
the progress of no life
living in the black box.

The Baby Singer

My mother called him a gypsy.
But he could make babies stop crying
even the colicky ones.
He came with a violin
played for babies and eagles—
He played lullabies with long, low tones that hummed
in the throat as crooning. Soon, the child would be silent
only breath echoed from the bassinet—
a backbeat to the willowy wind of a gypsy's violin—
the steady buzz of vibration on strings, just passing through
and the christians deemed him evil, dark and unsavory
offering sermons of warnings and protection
to young mothers and young women of how
spirit steals spirit and before you know it your loved ones
will get that look in their eyes, a look of knowing
that the power of god is born in all of us and god
loves to laugh, dance, sing and travel on the strings
of fiddles, zithers and hammer dulcimers—some times
in the form of skirts swirling elation or the sorrow sung
into the round mouths of caves traveling
to the womb and void of god giving birth
as a backbeat of breath whispering
from the mouth of a wicker bassinet.

Summer Photos with the Boys at the Creek

I would not let go of defiance in my straight neck
squared-off look-you-in-the-eye stare unlike Emmett's
knock-the-chip-off-my-shoulder cocked chin stare.

Mine was solid. The scar at the corner of my flat line lips
from the rim and tire iron incident made it so.

My chest is not out like Emmett's hit-me-first chest
so I can hit-you-back
hit you back
hit you back
hit you back.

My arms crossed, hands securely braced elbows into a square
the predictable square. Jack's lips were softer than mine. He held his hand
like a beggar. My defiance carried me
through the "incident" at Sunday school
and the medical exam designed for defiant girls
with Sunday school incidents.

I had to learn about the half-body of the subtle
the non-committed-stance of the half-a-thought
and those who inferred arrogance
toward those who didn't.

Fathers Gone

We were long legged gazelles waiting for the birth of a "melon"
called baby. The laundry is endless. The diaper pail
basks in the backyard behind the summer kitchen
amongst the kudzu and Spanish moss.
Taking a break from climbing trees
and scrappin' with the affluent white boys,
that gal Jessie pressed her first born status
upon the newest family creation, the newest family member.

The Wringer Washer—also a new edition, a luxury
to squeeze water from endless Birdseye diapers.
Soon
the birthing of an indoor washing machine
soon
the birthing will conclude like a string of pearls or watch fob of destiny
the oldest, the youngest, the unexpected.
This is a long legged clothesline that lopes
along the banks of slow moving Southern rivers
its pregnant swells breech over bankings—over levees,
to recede like a hairline,
or a hand from a black widow,
a foot from a copperhead—
recede from the overgrown summer kitchen full of canned goods,
children's battered toys,
a new diaper pail,
an absent father.

Recollections from My Law Office Window
—40 Floors Up

"You will not be spit on" Papa was diligent
"You will know numbers, know to write. You will read papers"
Papa was emphatic and sat right beside me
until my homework was complete.

I was not the oldest. I was the youngest. Sergio.
I wanted to be like Sergio. He was the oldest of us ten.
Papa made Sergio go to work with him
Mama said Sergio had to grow into it.

Sometimes Sergio, before he grew into it,
would beg Papa to go to school. He would do the chores too fast
run away to the teacher or to watch the girls.
Papa would always find out
Sergio paid the price with bruises—
the strap left long, purple lines even on Sergio's dark back.

I wanted to be like Sergio because Sergio was strong.
He grew into it, outworked everyone
Mama and Papa didn't have to work so much.
Sergio caught me skipping school once and
he beat me up in the barn. I tried to tell him
how I wanted to be strong like him.
I drank Sambuca. Smoked cigars. Puked for days.
I wanted my skin to be the sun-oil-dark like Sergio's rippled muscles.
Sergio's back hand cracked my face, spun me flying, snot and spit flung
he screamed 'til the veins popped out of his bull neck and skull,

"Do you think Papa was always an old man?!"
Sergio grabbed my head with his rough, square hands.
I smelt earth and tobacco. He looked me dead in the eye—
a young man already dead and he knew it—
the last man at the wall flinging others over to escape—

"Don't you ever let me catch you skipping school again
or I'll beat you crazy!"

Sons and Fathers—Brighton Beach

In the palm of his hand
I tried to be perfect and I was. My two sandaled feet
the width of his one great hand—my soles rooted
to his life line, mound of Venus, mound of Mars.
Held high, an acrobat stunt, or an offering to the Gods,
I was not afraid of him but perfect in his hand, face, smile—
our same curly hair—
my baby coat buttoned high with one round collar scalloping
my fat cheek. I grew and he had to use two hands
to keep me—one foot in each hand—his balance was my balance.
I grew and he used his feet on my hip bones to suspend me above him.
I grew and his hand supported my back to push me forward.
I grew and he placed his hands on my shoulders to slow me down.

We have the same ears but it was his brown eyes that held me
brought joy, sorrow, sharpness, and obsidian anger.
Taller, I grew, heavier,
still trying to be approved, to be perfect,
always wanting to be held high again
held that sacred again.

Crooked Nose

To the side of his swaybacked bed he rolls.
He fumbles for the light, its bolt

of nightshade glare cannonballs the wall, fireballs
'cross pumpkin pine floorboards, narrowly

escapes through the squint of venetian blinds.
Another belladonna morning

searching for belt loops, dry socks, and cigarettes.
Another body-bag-fog-pressed morning

bleeds his clouded mind to the edge
of a Stewart's Shop coffee cup and gray mystery.

His travel mug is a cauldron, a sink hole
of chelated fear, sediment of silt

coats the inside of his cup
the true flavor, he claims.

Shimmed betwixt his eyelids are the well kept
sleepy seeds of anger that wait, their coiled

chaos like morning datura with its luscious,
closed fluted tongue blossoms fleshy

lips of fragrance unraveling sunrise
into a pastoral oblique of greens

that spreads itself as a garden of toads
and slugs, moles and snakes, earthworms and beetles—

each hue cultivating the other, deft
is the hand that tills the syrian rue.

Cleft is the chin that harrows the air with arrogance
the air, the hummingbird swirls its slashing

wings, rises up as did twenty years ago
again and again, not dead like the sparrow

left under the leathery lobes of bloodroot
but resurrected through the "O" of it all.

The bambilia camouflaged his flaccidity.
Even then, too succulent as fit root

from a distance their opulence everlasting,
but snap: with the pressure of a pastelled touch

compression the color of fragrant bitter root.
Gravel along the brook reminds him of

the day he found the sparrow stiff
under the canopy of sanguinaria.

There was nothing to let go of but the flutter
of feathery hope a bird no longer needed him

to hold and twenty years ago it was abrasively
concrete as the thud heard as a car door slammed

but a bird to the windshield to the roadside had fallen
wings, capoeira in the dirt, bathing or dying or

fighting the resurrection that a child's laughter cultivates
until the weight of death itself presses back

the leaves the ancestors cloak their breath with.
No one wants to touch his world

betwixt the wavering gold grasses, fields of it,
and the underneath of his monkshood,

and fruitless may apple
where he toys with the idea of light.

Grampa's House

A man of structure—
black horn-rimmed glasses, a crew cut, boxtop, smiling—
In his chair in the sitting room-his back to the front, the street
and Cecil's general store.

My Dad and I would pull into the short driveway
and come in through the garage
on warm days, usually in summer
when it was still light and the birds still singing.

We would walk through the once-horse-stall-hog-pen-now-garage
into the tool shop—our shoed feet scuffed tin shavings and sawdust
under wooden work benches soaked with bar oil, pine
and cool dampness. We walked through another door
into the summer kitchen across the Andy Warhol linoleum,
through the scent of mothballs
our weight triggering like pressure plates
the pumpkin pine floorboards that rattled
the stacked tin buckets made
by Great-Great-Grampa Daniel from Scotland
and Grammy's bottle collection from years of dump digging adventures.

Plaid wool coats hung year round
to the left of the door into the main house that opened
only as far as the magnet coated refrigerator allowed
but just enough to look straight past Grammy's oak library desk,
African violets, spider plants and Christmas cactus—
open just enough to stocking-foot-slide
across the unplumbed hardwood dining room floors
causing green Wedgewood platters, plates, tureens to jostle like chimes

that tinkled from a swirling movement passed through a child's bare toes
like flying fingers reading brail, toes that skimmed and stumbled
across the topography of a braided rug and its woven, rural contours
of Grampa's repurposed red checkered wool coat
and deep forest green wool work pants still seasoned with pine pitch.

It is a child's world of tactile wonder and safety and recognition and
Grampa's beaming round face
behind the square black horn-rimmed glasses, the great bear paw hands,
It is the right way, the way things are supposed to be,
the throne of protection this laughing lap of Grampa.

Grandma's Revolution

"What's up?"
Mavis asked with a snap of her elasticized Kotex belt—
iconic historical feminine harness. Mavis had gone to a rally in 1961
a kind of protest—
she came back with short hair and new habits.

Mavis
didn't hesitate to walk about her apartment nude, smoking a cigarette,
her body an outrageous liberal pontification.
"What's up with this business of constant struggle?
My body is my own, look at me! A real person I don't have to be
like anyone."

Mavis
her palm toward the camera
there is movement in the movement launched
through decades of unrest
as liberation requires—
requires the sacrifice of blood that
Mavis knew
the history that always repeats itself.

Grandma Mavis
caused her great-granddaughters to blush
drove them to tweet in disgust the discovery
of Mod Mavis the Liberated.

Tweet. Twit. Blog. Instagram. Trend…all conducted from a mall
or couch or corner—only to imagine the surface
never below it, into it, discover it, taste it, consume it—

know nothing of the sacrifices
the lives
the blood

no, nothing—"hey what's up?"

Harvesting the Spring

I like the way sounds travel
from the backyard through partially opened kitchen windows
and the way barking dogs warbling tin-like yips
run between the up and down of screen mesh.

It's only March
but the sun is determined enough to warm river ice,
to make it sink below green water
that waits for the ritual ice floe.

I long for wild strawberries
and wait for frost heaves to flatten
and Earth for my feet to sink into.

Like Grampa's workhorse, Danny-Boy, in July or August,
long before midday Grampa and Danny would finish twitching logs,
down by the brook I'd find them,
Grampa slurping water from a tin can that usually hung on an Alder
and Danny letting water drizzle from his horse lips
standing to his cannons in cool mint mud.
He balked often when Grampa's tongue clicked.
Danny's anvil hooves pulled from the grasping ground,
reluctance in his plodding gate.
His muzzle whispered at Grampa's ear
and Grampa mumbled understanding,
his pace as slow as Danny's.

I long for wild strawberries and waterlilies, loons
and dirt to sink my feet into.
I always lost my shoes as a child

and before snow had cleared
from the thawing woods
I would sneak around our house to the backyard
where the Southern sun melted one spot
before anywhere else. I'd toe dance
through the corn snow
my bare feet hot to plant myself in the sprouting sod
until someone neighed angrily, "Where are your shoes?"

I long for wild strawberries
and the little girl
who used to pick them.

When Christ Was A Hustler

In between the rushes
a red petal glides
much like the return of an echo
pulled by the ear to be heard as a travel story,
carrying warnings, suggestions, dining tips...

When Christ was a hustler
it was Mary M. who kept his secrets
confirming his humanness. It was Mary M.
who touched him in ways that reaffirmed
he was still a man and the Son of God
at the same time.
It was Mary M. who held the power
of Gaia in her silence and dedication.

She laid among the stones, one of them
flies feasting on burgundy blood, dried, brushed along her hairline,
they buzzed between her reed-like fingers,
light upon the backs of her broken hands,
earth in her palms.
She had just used them days before
washing the Cloth of Christ.
What makes a good woman?

The art of love.
Mary M. smiled anointing his feet.
She knew what not to say and listened
to his breath change to sleep, color flowed into his face—
washed away all humanness from his forehead and cheeks.
He slept soundly

and rose free of the chains of betrayal.

"A miracle" she thought,
the power of God in her hands.

Imminent Domain

Aunt Sophie's son stole my tricycle.
Older, bigger, swaggering his male favoritism,
I relinquished the tricycle
too small for my cousin's display of arrogance there on the tarmac
in blistering July.

My Mother taught me different. My Mother,
who protected Aunt Sophie's kids from stray men in fancy cars,
had chased more than one man with an ax
loaded another full of birdshot. I was taught
to keep quiet, wait for your moment.

We were raised different
unobtrusively I turned on the outdoor spigot, grabbed the nozzled hose,
and blasted him—sent him screeching
for Aunt Sophie's underskirts.

Like a struck hornet filled piñata women emerged from the house.
Water off, hose recoiled, with repose and calm, I pedaled my tricycle.
Furious, Aunt Sophie railed—How dare I, a small female thing,
tongue tied from head injuries, have the audacity to attack her son?

My mother watched.
I gazed, paused the squawking pedals and stated,
"He took my tricycle. I took it back."

Umbra

Papa's necklace glowed gold and round
umbrated by the shadow of olive leaves.
Mama gave that necklace to him.
We scrunched our eyes
waiting for the sun to go dark
I was eclipsed by Papa's Adam's apple and his thick hand
on my frail shoulder and Sunday sweater, eclipsed
by Mama's absence—

I wondered
was she in the shade of the shadowed doorframe?
Was she betwixt the bricks and two by fours?
Was she in Papa's pocket, his twill trousers and suit jacket?

An event
this eclipse
like a slap to the head.
Why do people die and where do they go?

Papa works harder now—his shirt is clean
we took this time, today, he said, because maybe
the Mamas go behind the sun.

I scrunch and twist my eyes, twist my nose
I skewed my mouth in this picture
because I wanted to help ease Papa's sorrow.

The gold coin on his throat shone remembrance of love, a gift
that maybe, if I stood still enough,
and like the shadow of St. Timothy passing over my Papa and me

we could get on with our lives
and Mama could get on with hers.

That photo was taken fifty years ago.
Papa's hand still touches my shoulder
the gold chain remains a brilliant drop, a super nova,
my Mother's striking light of immortality.

Ghost Photo

The linoleum is eggplant purple, worn
and hot from the woodstove in the cellar
white streaks, nebulous shapes
splash the kitchen floor sprinkled with bread flour.

She rode a tricycle,
a hand-me-down through six children.
Its tires split with age stuck somewhat
to the kitchen's art deco floor. When freshly waxed
it buckled, and creaked.
Her hair was Protestant orange.

The child was topless pedaling sternly
in and out of rooms and points of view. Years later
her hair was not so orange. Her spirit
annealed the flames into strong shoulders, taught breasts.
The linoleum was torn-up, waxed, and used as sleds
down the backyard iced sliding ramp.

The linoleum
never washed clean.

Childhood Names

"Mumma, what's a Hesperus?"
I asked in response to my mother's statement, "Suzy,
you have the luck of the Hesperus."

Who is Jezebel? What's a Banshee? And why do they scream?

Mysteries blown away with the rustle of late August grasses
in the old pasture and apple orchard
'cross from Spike Knowles's shanty on the intervale.
"Spike" is what Mumma told us kids to call him
even though we knew everyone else called him "kike"
even though we had no idea what that meant.

We knew that Spike didn't have a car
and still went to town with his team of horses and buckboard wagon.
Us kids would listen for the absorbed jingle of bone harness rings
their ghostly arrival—sounded before seen—
pulled forward by the draft of a Mercury Comet.
Starving-child-wide-eyed waiting at the roadside
we'd hail the past through our present parade.
Mumma brought him water.
Carrots for the team and we got to feed and pet their magnificence—
The smell of oats, molasses, saddle soap, and horse.

Spike knew everybody 'cause he owned the big swimming hole
that had the fat leeches and long red-bellied bloodsuckers
that you had to remove with a strand of hair or tons of salt.
One of the round ones had babies between my toes. My brother and I
watched it in the back of the high-tail-finned Plymouth wagon
before dousing them with fiery alkalinity.

We'd ride our bicycles five miles or so, spin the bottle,
and run like bare-assed Banshees through the pasture
and wrap like tight curled wind devils around ancient apple trees
their gnarled knuckled Dante roots grabbed our feet and legs
sprawled us flat to the Earth, so close, we'd snort like deer and bear
the chaff and aphids from our mouths and noses. Our hands
slapped the ground like wrestlers and we'd smash rotten apples—
prized ammo for stick apple fights—sun-fermented apples worked best
when snapped mercilessly from the tip of a sucker switch
splattered our backs like buckshot
left bruises and stains the bees swarmed.
Our screams cut sharp paths through late August grass blazing zigzags
to the safety of our swimming hole
and its convex outcrops of stone treachery,
swamp alder barriers protected us from roadside viewing.

We'd race back home on bicycles
hair and towels flapped wildly
tucking chin, head and elbows in for the final descent
down the hill by the school house hug tight right into the driveway
for a flying dismount by the back porch
a decisive moment of who won
and my Mother's kiai,
"JEZEBEL! Have you been playing with those boys again?!"

Bitty's Baby Doll

The summer temperatures were running in the high nineties.
No one slept with clothing on
blankets of humidity pressed into creased flesh
like lint between toes, under armpits, behind knees.

No Papa. Just Mumma, sisters and one bed.
We all slept in one bed, a donated luxury, and me, being the oldest,
was up before the others
except for Mumma who was up first
drinking her first coffee
smoking her first Tareyton extra-long.

Mornings felt no different than night, an unchanged condition,
marked only by Mumma's occasional blackeye and
Bitty's bad habit of pissin' the bed.
Mumma couldn't have men over if the mattress was wet.

Air never dry enough to dry the piss
from a shame-stained mattress.
Rancidity is bitter like the way Mumma's jaw set tight
causing her mouth to flatline razor thin

except for that one corner that clenched
a bouncing cigarette conducting blame
through those balloons squealing thin lips
because Bitty pissed the bed, again,

and how we'd all go without food, again, and how
it was my fault, again, and how
Bitty's baby doll always fell out of bed, again—

again, again until our ragdoll hearts
lay mildewed and limp until
the schoolteacher found a colony
of baby cockroaches in the soles of my rotten sneakers
until Bitty talked to the school nurse
about how she could kill herself by stepping in front of the train
at the corner of Palmer and Main, just like Mumma said she could.

Photo Vignette # 2

Andy and Jeb
moved into the old milk house because it was already wired for lights
It was already
a hot June and the cinderblocks stayed cool. It was hard
to imagine carpets of any kind on concrete, no screens,
and some kind of crazy hope
that even Andy in her "new beginnings" naiveté could see
looking back
at the first photo of her and Jeb at the milk house.

Jeb was a plain man with hard boundaries.
His expectations of Andy were uncomplicated and rigid.
Toward the end, when the photo was taken, she turned her head away—
slapped by the space between them. So typical,
for her to reach for him.

Jeb was a laborer. Worked even when he was sick
but forgot too many of the little things. Andy realized
Jeb was like the concrete blocks and she
more like the mortar
even mortar cracks with stress, age, and pounding.

Summer Vacation

The creek's clay-green water moved slowly as a reprieve
from the rush hour traffic that Amanda, from Manhattan,
spoke dramatically about through the space between her teeth
and around the soda straw she wedged there.
She insisted on Diet Coke and found skinny-dipping ludicrous,
simply insane. Marjorie, on the other hand,
on the other side of the tin TV table, expressed her nudity
in the arabesque arching of her long torso and flat chest
not even a pubic hair—her toes leading point
as she walked the camp porch rail as a balance beam.
Marjorie enjoyed playing cards. Actually, she enjoyed most
the easy transition from teetering on thin rails to the tactility
and finesse of the fingers of her left hand fanning the cards
while the right hand placed her selected card—forefinger and thumb—
with a deliberate snap on the flimsy TV table with hollow legs.
That's what Marjorie liked sitting in the frayed lawn chair
on the shaded camp deck.

Amanda enjoyed mouthing the straw
and discussing the unknown possibilities of a new deck of cards
and sneaking cigarettes with the older boys
under the bridge further down the creek,

Amanda would recall Missouri ten years later
showering repeatedly
to wash the smell of the unknown from her body.
She would add rum to her Coke
to keep the unknown from penetrating her consciousness.
She would light cigarettes, jiggle her flimsy legs
and not recall the color of the creek.

The Next Time

It was a reincarnation not to be expected but to endure.
There were turrets of personalities and mental disorders
that broke into babble.
Living with the mentally ill is like riding in a loose saddle—
there are no reins of reason and nothing is a cinch
just needs
to be met at whatever expense is necessary.

The direction
the moments of stars bright
Christmas candies of cruelty
dissolve leaving thirst.

It is hard to love moments.
It is hard to love.

Not Tonight

I offer you the hand that is dangling
off the stainless-steel table, distorted
by thin sheets or gauze or nervousness shaking a camera.

The curve of a buttocks will miss this hand
this hand cracked with sheetrock and plaster,
the thickness of labor and short lifelines.

A jaw will miss the cupping of this hand
manicured by wrenches and softened by children.

Kelsey's bar will miss this hand
slapping down a five and sucking down a draft.

There is
at the corner of Howard and Contralto Streets
a brown house with beige shutters and a small woman
by the front stoop watering begonias
who has not yet received a phone call
and she is still singing a song the hand
would wave the tempo to and pat her breasts then
draw a line from her forehead to the edge
of her panties and the soft
lips above her inner thigh
on the way home from Kelsey's.

Iron Novena

A small burl. A Danish pipe.
He worked for the railroad in Arizona
taking with him his dark-grained pipe with natural edges.
He rode the train this time every year for seventy-five years now.
His knotted knuckles recalled jolts of impact
from setting railroad stakes—tons of iron—

An old man now
streaked skyline—fresh paint young—
the sunset saturated the silhouette of saguaro cactus,
prickly pear, and cholla.

He lit his pipe biting the end
his jaw tightened, at ten miles out John lost his arm,
Ben dropped dead from heat and sun,
Sonny stayed strong 'till they went to town—
Practical recollections: what he held in his hands
was the fruit of dust, the dawn of smoke, the strike of iron,
the power of memory of men in their youth
laying tracks that cut through sand,
that cut away gnarled scrub brush
splayed open the bones of truth
of how many died for progress
the wheels still clack
he empties the ash
recites their names
an incantation
a rosary of men.

When Daddies Play

I weep at the sight of a caricature, a cartoon, a positive-negative,
a white silhouette of Charlie Chaplin
holding the hand of a child.
They are walking somewhere up stone steps into rectangles of light.

I weep when I view photos of us squinting our eyes at the sun.
I weep at knowing too much.
I weep at the logic of shoot-to-kill.
I weep at seeing Daddies throw their babies high into the air,
no matter where in the world
all Daddies throw babies to the sky
and everybody laughs.

I weep when I see Daddies make their children feel smaller
than what they know
they already are.

I weep remembering Daddies wiping tears from their face
when they load the rifle
to kill the animals
that we can't fix.

The Execution

This is the photograph that I grew up with.
The photograph in black and white, Nguyễn Văn Lém, Việt Cộng,
hands tied behind his back
Saigon, Smith & Wesson .38 to his right temple, standing
he lists slightly away—his eyes squeezed tight as folded paper fans
his mouth contracts bracing—he knows
that knowing his prayers are useless, is useless.
The General has already taken aim.

This was before color TV, computers were fantasy,
a plaid shirt, jungle greens, a mass grave, a Pulitzer prize...
How the world changed: Did it?

The apocalyptic dawn and dusk
thins like weighted discs between vertebrae.
Violence is a heavy thing.
It is a burqa with a politician's lead hem
drawing the gravitational tug of war through the shit
through the thick viscera of shoulders, torso, back of legs, soles of feet—
it is a stole of .50 cal ammo rounding the soldiers of time—
a pendulum of carcass hung from a bridge in Fallujah
dowsing the Euphrates.

...Xbox, Wii, Nintendo, YouTube...What is real? What is not?
It was real for the man whose exit wound took half his head.
It was real for the man who pulled the trigger.
It was real for the camera man who kept shooting a frame
that he sees over and over and over forty years later
I spotted just a corner of this photo
from under a pile of rough-edged pages

a coffee table edition of History Americana—
as real today as it was then.
And most who read this
will not know what I'm talking about.
But some of you
you know this photo
you know these places
as clear as I.
It is in our fiber.

You will remember, won't you? Won't you?

In this Water

A cul-de-sac caution sign—an incessant
flash of warning lights—

Is this it? My last word? My last poem? The last
tingling over left cheekbone trigeminal nerve—
a Morse code trickling through shiny gray wires
to a deep-water shelf
where only little girls swimming with sharks, octopi, and stingrays
can breathe into a pillow of gills
gasp for life
I cannot speak of the world beyond the drowning
beyond
the body of this world
the rest of the world
calls a fantasy
so this little girl, this little me, presses her koi lips
into the airless weight of foam and silence and submerges
her ears below the water line
listening with an aquatic heart to the insulated wonder
of the secrets of regrets, remorse, requiems of guilt tangled
in the trundling hair loose as seagrasses
on the edge of her world
lying on the sand bottom
looking up through the tunnel of light,
the hole in the sky,
the war of tides.

Survivability

She was always more defiant than me.
Mumma blamed her for teaching me
how to put my hands on my hips.
Because I was too young to smoke
I was pissed off
and climbed trees like a boy, got pitch
all through my hair, "a wild thing" my father said
but it was Mumma who cut my hair
because she had run out of Lestoil.

I was pissed off
about the dangerous-treads-worn-off-red-rubber-boots that Mumma
took to the outdoor burn-barrel way down back behind the house
four years old
I dragged myself through the January snow
stood up beside the burn-barrel, didn't fall in
and claimed my boots.

My cropped hair got pinned curled with crisscrossed
plastic coated bobby pins. That summer was hot
us kids "ran like beggahs" Mumma said.
We snuck matches and cigs. I was too young to smoke
and stood guard. There was solidarity in our defiance.
My sister marched in anti-war protests
She wore the first mini skirt to high school.
Mumma gave me my first knife.
I joined the Marine Corps.

II

silencer

keeper of secrets
never tell on the men
acknowledge my knowledge
this is my darkness
this is my gun

Palmetto

Parris Island, South Carolina sand is fine
like Camp Edwards like powder like dust
like makeup from round, metal saucer discs
with a compact mirror to reflect the shine
or dark circles or crow's feet
or three sisters posing in Summer Dress Greens
standing under Palmettos in historic Beaufort
before, before, before…
Morales, Rasmussen, Baumgardner

after I was raped

an incidental Army man from Cleveland Heights with dark eyes, hair,
round head and a regulation mustache
sat with me on the WWII concrete barrack's porch.
he had heard what happened.
we drank liquor.
he was safe.
his tawny eyelids half-closed—silent—the oppressive Indiana July air
thick with premonitions—tornadoes to come—my life—
he drew a quick breath through square white teeth,
ticked his head with a jerk
wrinkling the flesh of his olive-skinned neck
in a graveled moan he murmured,
  "Oh, Zsuska, Zsuska,"

No Daddies

What kind of fantasies
do little boys have who have no Daddies?

Who are the fathers that had no fathers
that ran away
from Alpha Daddies
who beat them down into corners of absence?

Run
Run far and fast away
from fear that your Daddies' rage and hatred
has metastasized into more sons without fathers.

It can't be, just can't be.
If only you had more power.

Iron Umbrella

I don't know this man and his children.
It is the first time we have met.
The umbrella is a luxury of shade for the innocent
a shield against the rain of trauma
that took his wife—their mother.
The burden of war is strapped to the backs of the survivors.
The bundle of the future transferred from hip to spine to shoulder
cradling an M16, AK, RPG, SAW.
An umbrella
is a starry structured shield against the rain of plutonium, radium.
The father knows his oldest son—still a toddler—
already knows that drops of rain like drops of lies
accumulate into puddles, rivulets, floods
that wash away the beauty of a strong arm
an infant's utterance

The Hunt

I'm not sure
where the ride was supposed to take me.
I look to the sky a lot lately.

How docile the Blackhawks are
at the hanger. Like dogs in the pen,
the Blackhawks' matt finish soaks up the sun
their hound dog props pick up to attention
at the sound of clips, bolts, boots.

The Negative

I am a little girl.
My hair is not cut or combed but my father knows me.
I don't speak your language—these are my thoughts.

My father lets me hold him because he knows I am afraid.
I know he is afraid.
My ear is pressed to his chest and I hear his heart beating
he is ready to protect me— his body is tight
he raises up in his spine
a striking snake taking aim.

There is a man—
I have never seen skin with no color
but my father has and the men
tell stories of the hard times that follow
the visits of the no-color-skin-people. This man
has something like a box he presses to his face.
He speaks his language from behind the box, his mask—
the man squeezes the box—a click sound comes from inside.
The sick-skin-man takes his mask off—
smiles, makes his language sounds
he is happy with his box-mask.

My father holds me closer. He says
the sick-skin-man brought my clothing that we are forced to wear.
My father refuses to cover his sun and earth toughened flesh.
He still sits squatting close to the earth.
I am afraid. I don't like the sick-skin-man.
My father glares hard from under his weathered wrinkles
intensely deep from sun and knowing.

My father knows something about the sick-skin-man.
I don't like him or his box that is taking something away from me—
this box that he holds to his face like a mask
with hands too clean—fingers too soft.

Tsunami Conflict

from a beach in Vietnam
a young soldier plucked a shell—
the remains of a white shell—
a spiraled-nautilus-breast-shaped-round shell
that he carried back to the jungle
of night's death, surreality of rotting flesh—
a camaraderie of confusion.

the soldier's thumb
fits into the underside of curves and topical ridges
an inverted nipple
a confluence of politics
a paradox of ethics
that he carries in his rucksack
and M-16.

an old man—an old woman—
the soldier—the shell—
children—gains—losses
washing across beaches
his thumb still in the shell
still tracing
the topography of survival.

Visions of Clara

In the shadows of the guardrails he sat on a box
in the dirt shoulder— his camo parka unzipped, flapped
like crow's wings hopping toward roadkill,
victims of landmines and ambush.

He was anxious for a ride that never stopped. His moment
out of context. His mind left behind in sand
and hot shells, rounds emptied, burning jeeps—
His eyes were excited by visions or tanks or
flags flapping like his coat and metal zipper pulls
tinkling like dog-tags. He was not in Tennessee.
Who is Clara? Who was he?

He was anxious for a ride that never stopped. A destination
that never arrived but only in night sweats
and screams—Next Of Kin—where is Clara?
He could not be touched and didn't know why—N.O.K.—
where is Clara?

BA BOOM

at the crux of four chambers
there is enough stillness to move
in any direction—a chambered round
fired downrange in a direction
of passion or survival

what is action?

I was just saying the other day
how some assaults
cause one person to disintegrate into wicked submission
and others rise with horrific glorification
from the fields of shadows
burn as wild-fired stars—
lightning bolts of steel

march regression
into cavities of accountability
reload the heart
with shells of Bright—Bright integrity

Reenlistment – the Global War on Terror

Keys in our hands, words from our mouths
murmuring oaths, brandishing gallantry

Kindness is a brushing branch
compassion the morning sun piercing pine needles
anchored by dew

It is ancient
this calling roar exploding from the assadic heart
this doorway

does not lead to safety
before harsh fires, before microbursts of violent cadence,
before the silence of not giving

a rabbit, half brown, half white, with loose tufts of winter
hops from under the accumulation of sprills
pauses for scents on which to graze its nose

it is a hard horse to ride, this wind,
a thousand years, it takes, to turn around

The Golden Hour

one one-thousand, two one-thousand, three one-thousand...

the second hand sweeps phosphorous cardinal numbers
faux reptilian strap holds a rectangular face—fun house mirror
        distortion—
under a domed crystal

four one-thousand, five one-thousand, six one-thousand...

i would not have purchased this watch
the woman who owned this watch did not wear it often—
she was not a medic, nurse, or health care specialist

seven one-thousand, eight one-thousand, nine one-thousand...

how long has it been
since there was a pulse in my wrist worthy of vitality?
stories are vital. recognition is vital. validation is vital.
isolation is only part of the story

ten one-thousand, eleven one-thousand...

The Shortest Day Before the Light

A Borscht day of stacking wood. Every fiber of myself burns, every
cell pounds with pulverized and soured mashed pain.
A Solstice in wet purple suede gloves the dye rendered my hands
a chilblain red—each crease parenthesized each knuckle
each clenched mound of passing, a vertebral rosary, Ranger Beads ticked,
each stick of wood stacked.

It doesn't matter—the rain, the snow, the sweat—I'm struck
by my own purple hands
and how the depth of my palms clutch
the untainted brilliance—
refuse to dye—
my jagged lines of heart and life.

Against All Enemies—Foreign and Domestic

Music too loud, too sharp, stab my pineal—
my reflexive hands grasp for my sword and Pipe.

My brain's load shifts and topples
the weight of unknown leverage—too late to stop
my rage stuck like a dragonfly, moth or butterfly
betwixt air filter and valves, a friggin' wedge of brittle
glassed wings forced—held open—the air flow of brain and body
with a mix of emotions too rich with substance

I wanted to kill you
assailant
because you violated my home—my body.
You made my hands tremor for my weapon
set down for the sacred
and profane

I wanted to kill you
assailant
because your assault door-breached my leveed rage
broke open walled stanchions
of violent rape ragged memories surged relentless
flooded my brain with justified right action

Gates of Ur

In Old Quebec it began. Well, no,
that's not true. I would find things in the woods.
I would see archways and secret worlds of moss,
Lady Slippers and springs.
I would come home telling stories of little people
taking me into spiraling caves, and sinkholes. What felt like minutes
became hours. I could never find these places the next day.
The archways gone. Flowers gone.

In Santiago de Cuba I peered through thick adobe walls.
White bedsheets, sun bleached, billowed in courtyards
hung brightly on weathered rope clotheslines. Crisp
against tile floors, geometrically juxtaposed against Siboney blue sky,
shekeres, snap of la saya, kiss of Eleggua.

How did I learn to cry soundlessly?

To keep secret the alienation, the sensitivities,
the language of trees, stones, and spirit—
To keep voiceless the betrayal of lovers, the loss of innocence.
To keep still any movement of distraction or stir emotion's memories
like the late summer day when us kids watched
through the wide band of light when we slid the barndoor open
and witnessed the castration of bulls, straight-razors, whiskey, blood
and balls flung to the rafters.

How did I learn to cry soundlessly?

Why did they have to beat my cousin to death and not even take her
        money?

"She fought" the coroner said, "every bone in her hands and face were
        shattered,
        simply shattered!"
Why did my ex-husband keep us up till 3a.m. threatening to kill us all
        in our sleep?

I have walked through doorway after expansive doorway—
rage is a silencer on a 9mm.

I really do want to speak of sun, sand, ocean, and aromatic coffees.
I really do want a house with a pink door and stucco blue walls,
even chickens like Pepere—
bourbon, barley, champion gamecocks, and cigars—
There are some doors
I need to close.

Nectar's Photograph: Sandinista Fruit

fight for the cause. how can that be?
the men remove their hats, respect for the dead
but their bandoliers remained— crossed their hearts.
antonio had fallen. a comrade had fallen. a warrior had fallen.
rosalita now has no husband, her children no father. their future
trickles to a halt like
the drying blood from the corner of antonio's mouth.
mamacita has no son. he has fallen at the foot of the great tree
at the roots of the great tree. the seasons
will cover him with browned petals and wind swept leaves.
they call him a warrior.

the tree blossoms and bears fruit.
the tree continues to blossom and bear fruit.
the women cover their faces in mourning
the face of men exposed bright like brass shell casings.

silence
as though life produced itself
pressing grief
the weight of itself
the ancestral tree— its girth—
the circumference of all fruit
bearing itself
to become the fallen.

Fallout

I remember as a teen the whispers
in Hodgkin's General Store
the names of sons still in Vietnam,
whose sons came home in a bag.
I know Walter Cronkite for numbers dead, wounded, and missing.
Something I never wanted my sons to know.

No one seems to notice the buzz of bees
as they hum and dance through the depths of Amaranth buds.
No one seems to notice the fighter jets flying below radar
or the length of silence swept between jets two and three
a broom of overwatch waiting for a cloudburst
of lightning bolts and hail, twisters and justice
that strafe the plains of finance
like two young Eagles entangled in ejaculation
failing to count the milliseconds.

There Are No Wrong Numbers

I'm sorry I didn't know you.
It was late—I was still vacuuming at 11p.m.
I'd worked all day—the kids stayed up too late.
I'd made a dump run, cleaned the porch, done the dishes, twice.
Why were you surprised I wasn't asleep?
Your voice was weak and long distant.
I barely heard you over the dishwasher.

But I wanted to know who it was you wanted to hear.
Who it was you gentled your voice for.
Someone you loved? Someone
you wanted to press your belly to back with?
I wanted to know if you were married, had a lover, children—
If you were a man that needed things that didn't need you—
If you were the kind of man that got angry swatting houseflies
that never landed
and why it was you sounded disappointed and doubting
when I said I didn't know you
because I wanted to, I needed to
but you left no name, no number,
and you never called back.

Scottish Voice

her skin smelled of calendula and mallows
his of wintergreen
their hearts smoldered passion
their tongues want for flame

and in the cool of hunger
and desire to be fed
their souls wove a tapestry
of ancient silver threads

where might they have loved each other last?
in which age past did both drink life
where boyish fingers nudged her breasts
and gentled hands did search his groin?

where last his mouth suckled her neck
this breath that ne'er did dry
that sowed such summer fragrances
with sounds of rushing pine?

when last his face brushed hers, June supple fern,
her eyes slept with hope
where souls together wove
an ageless rope of time?

when last as vapors sweet the sun did scatter
knowin' not where they'd mix again—
did God's finger stir the clouds
of calendula, mallows, and wintergreen?

The Shepard's Star

gold heart Brahman
cascade of pearls
surround a beggar
on a universal street corner
plays a love song on a blues harp
he knows the chords as old kisses
still fresh on lip and tongue
with eyes closed
his breath lullabies the love he lost
nested in January's black abyss heaven

When We Were Close

This is how I carried your trauma.

The first time I slept with you
I woke screaming with sweat,
I couldn't breathe—
the other world still gripped inside me, the other world
jungle's humidity and sounds, Huey blew my hair back,
threw bones, blood, dust, and nightmares
into my eyes, ears, mouth, and nose.

"Vietnam," you said,
left you combat wounded, hating mosquitoes, and screaming children.
I remember
when you ran out of the mall in Jersey City,
a child's screams ricocheted
from floor to glass ceiling, off windows and into your head,
into your head
into your head.

Fear and death stain any uniform
changes the essence of anyone's skin.

The Tea Leaves Reader

Loose and dark the jasmine tea was.
With each clear breath I must drink to the dregs
flip the tea cup upside down
look at life from a different perspective.

I met a man once, she says, who held me like china
his presence was a query that desired to be drank
to the bottom of his soul, to turn his life around, to decipher
the symbolism in his relationships.

I wanted to cup my hands around his face, she says,
hold his cheekbones as well-crafted stoneware—savor the heat—
the fragrance of emotion, just a feeling, she says,
the needs that poured from his eyes.

Before the Wheel – Primitive Skills Workshop at Poke-O-Moonshine

the cold added cracks to my hands
that held the black of charred wood and ash
i knelt on the ground, moccasin lacing dug into the Earth
chest flat on the soil as flat as my pressing palms, elbow bent,
my right cheek brushed the peated dirt teased the tongue of frost.

you twisted the hand drill my breath spiraled around. the drill squawked.
your palms together prayed ferocity from the top of the drill
to a tuft of shredded cedar we prayed would burn a passion igniting
a recollection,
a smoldering memory my breath gentle across your knuckles
you were sweating and we prayed for life
as though it were past, present, and future—our lives depended on this
you on your knees, a convergence of humility, waiting for god
Fire.

flames

my tongue along your backbone runs
burns slow it knows
each vertebra as it knows
the marrow
the sizzling cordite of fuse

Pastries on Lark Street

My mother would sit here
delighted with the spotless glass tabletops
and their explosive glint of one-dimensionality
accented by the white-sugar-sand Zen-garden
artistically raked to correct depth.

Like unsuspecting backlight
I sit at a high-top table spying the front display window
and the melting wedding cake adorned with a wilted glaze
of sugar daffodils and crocus heads.

My mother would wear open-toed pumps
her nails painted crisply, a ponderance of moments,
not usually drinking espresso in the afternoon,
she would not resist the porcelain nostalgia of white demitasse and
saucer nesting a decadent fudge pastry graced
by an exclamation point of sterling silver dessert fork
supported by an extended non-linear garland of
gold wedding cakes with bells drizzled
around the rim of the bone china saucer.

The rum raisin flesh of a high maintenance chick, my Mother,
would sit at this high-top table eating pastries on Lark Street
because she would know that her presence
was accent to the immaculate floor
her elegance the polish of glass table tops
her honey tongue the glaze of fine Italian pastries
her eyes the cherry depth to dark chocolate
her vitality—stiff froth
her heart—bitter to the bean with a hint of Parodi.

The Brush

He touched her as though it were an accident, unintended calligraphy,
an accident that they were still lovers, he had not intended
that they would still be together and caught
by surprise he cultivated a vine of lies, subtleties of deception,
ink spatters of Rorschach.

Their "marriage" became a Tiamat of wandering shadows
false gestures in the name of convenience.

How close to death can you threaten light?
It made him feel
just enough.

She wondered
about mist leaking its way along the river's surface
through glacial heaves. She wondered
how some men hide their sexual abuse
and pound stones like flesh like pulp
into paper to tell stories of tragedy, accidents, fear
the cutting down of every thing
alive and loving
to justify the self-inflicted
dehumanization
desertion
rage

The Edge

I remember when you were the jewels of night and passion
and lightning bugs and I held your gestures
as treasure and your lies like splinters
festering in the bottom of my feet.

We had walked together   always denying together
always missing   together.
You were the brocade and rocaille beads of sweat
blood tests after blood tests
when positive means negative.

You were the passion of lightning bugs and wonder
and the little boy made to spread your cheeks and say you loved him
from there
you stopped loving yourself and began hating the world.

I held your gestures as treasure
and your lies like splinters.

Fanning Fire

Damn. I knew I should have vacuumed.
My mother always vacuumed
despite five kids who always had five friends,
a couple of dogs, cats and my dad's work boots.

My mother was ahead of her time or in denial or
chose escapism or was simply drunk. I don't care. She played
with us kids on her clean floors, finally clean floors. She had a house
with clean floors. While she laid on her back
she would place her narrow feet on my hip bones
our fingertips touching—ground eagle, sky eagle—
wingspan to wingspan, "Fly, Suzy, fly!"

I soared beyond her rages and whipping yardsticks.

The grass on the middle lawn was thick like golf courses,
a carpet most plush by the brick fireplace
never mortared never made permanent
the snakes nested there.
Mumma and I sat there and the snakes would come.
"This is how you hold them," her hand steady and direct
her voice unwavering. We would take turns holding the snakes,
look them in the eyes and not be afraid
of their wild beauty.

Between Harvest and Spring

I walk these fields alone
the first year is never easy
not enough distance between the rows
of memories and emotions
not enough hard rains
to wear down the hills
of diligently tilled soil
to wash away the unevenness of my heart
to make smooth again
the grief.

I guess you were a farmer.
Always yearning to get your hands in the dirt
always
needing to make grow—the dream
of getting out from behind the plow
to step back and admire
that which you cultivated.

I walk these fields alone
only to recall
hope's heavy fragrance
and the Earth
you once nurtured.

Venom, Sweet Venom

Who are you?
A lover drowned by ego? A husband? A river?
Oh, fragrant pain, moistened dew of desire to be something
you were afraid of becoming.

If I didn't know better I would think you never existed
but for the petaled-bruised magnolia flesh that could not be touched
the oxidation of swirls and whorls of fingerprints rising up
to the surface, proof, that touching of some kind occurred in your
crazy, confused life.

My sorrowful bucket gut roils with questions: who are you in this
       moment
telling people a piece of the story like serving a slice of pie
but never the whole pie.

Only in moments of recollections can the wholeness be reassembled
with the pulling of each berry seed, hull, and stem
from teeth, palette, and throat.

Fragments. Together. Apart. Together. Apart.

You were a flower
whose euphoric fragrance
was as hypnotic and numbing as a spider bite.
I emptied myself
into your poison.

So Many Selves

It is a crowded bus in a star-riddled black night,
sand fleas, black flag days.
It is a cattle car we stood in
shoulder to shoulder jostled like soda bottles in wooden crates
canteens on web belts on young hips sloshed.

There was the loud self, the nonsense self, the mother self,
the fleeting self
like autumn leaves twirling into torrents of dirt devils
dispersing into scattered calm self that placed a foot into a left and right
boot of quick lace black eyelets mountain gal survivor self.

Lost lovers self, ex-husband selves, drunken self, determined self.
A joist of connectedness
geometric selves, multifaceted dynamic blue diamond self.
Only the tanned-skinned sun self
can melt into any sense at all these selves
have become micro millennia of evolution
of the self that I view, on occasion, as a diorama,
not straightforward like the wooden hand-held gadget that Grammie
let us put post cards in
and we peered through the bubble glass eyepieces
pretending we were everywhere
but in the front room, cold, and waiting for hot pie self.

a dove is not

a beehive of stitched rocaille, a round box oxymoron
of braided wire ravishing pink with one, ruby centered
nippled-eye for a lid.
Inside, a black velvet nest harbors a white dove
bezeled by turquoise, brown and white seed beads
a pin, it is,
to appliqué to a beret to a collar to a shoulder
to a ribbon of thought—
a brocade statement released Pandorically
replaced with my silenced conundrum
that cannot feed doves
that cannot live
off words of rescue never spoken
snuffed out by a capped lid
twisted tight.

Ghost Nets

I was tall for fourteen when the bombs dropped like spider bites
along the shoreline. Our thatched huts and boats flew
in pieces, bone fragments, body parts, and humanity
hurdled through the gossamer of politics.

My father sat holding a few scraps of paper and photos
that survived unscathed as miraculously
as our own survival. Nothing moved
but the smoke and steam weaving between the stalks
of blasted boat dock supports and dead fish. There was no one.

Everything in that moment became ghosts. Even us.
I lost my mother, aunts, sisters, brothers, and most of my father
but we knew we would survive. We already had.
It was the devastation that hollowed us like pigs prepped for roasting.
My father stuffed himself with ghosts.
My emptiness became a boat and I fished for souls
I made nets to cast until I caught new dreams to live.

Opening

Some grains of wood darken with age.
Such objects linger like woodsmoke on your wool, plaid jacket
or your hair when it gets wet in the shower after tending fires,
burn pits, sometimes JP5, or JP8, sometimes worse.

This box holds fires and smoke and embers
and the hummingbird effigy pulling nectar from the star of creation
in a circle that encapsulates cycles, your brand, you said
pressing the small iron into wood with a soft hiss and swirl of smoke.

The red oak grains are the wind waves of White Sands —
they are growth lines in trees whose silence is cross-sectioned
with inquiry and self-doubt like our coast to coast summer vacation
stranded at White Sands hovering in sparse shadows waiting
for the circling Blackbird 71s to go full throttle, bust the sky
their jet fuel, a mirage, settled onto the White Sand,
our vacation, our marriage, someone else's sons.

I don't open this box often.
There is a crack in the bottom of the smaller than a thimble basket—
after twenty years it checks.
The turquoise tooth fits in it—the basket cradles the jagged edge—
exposes a white center like the hull of a corn kernel
still stuck between the teeth.

This box is a little coffin lined with red velvet
recycled from someone's great-great-grandmother's
loveseat upholstery upon which sits
the broken tooth of turquoise and an empty
peach pit basket that stands on its own.

Your love for me did not. Nor mine for you.

Nesting Dolls of memories inside of events,
emotions inside of memories, indecisiveness inside of emotions—
You never could make up your mind and often recounted
stories as a boy you couldn't decide to stay or go.

In the middle of the upper Hudson
shards of whitewater refracted a billion illumines of sun
your heart exploded

Geisha On Vacation

Wipe the wet bird shit off the Adirondack chair.
Morning still
the whistle of birds emphasize their hustle.

To quiet her mouth, she applies lipstick to her upper lip, not red,
earth brown with gold silica sparkles—mud murmuring
a slurry of ancestral reckoning.

A bluebird flutters through branches,
its Creamsicle breast poised front and center
she rubs her unpainted neck.

"I told you so," the wind said
brushing her eyes with a twirling spindle of her own hair.
It was expensive lipstick—she realizes now
the cost of silence.

The Whipple Tree[1] of Fate

Just before noon
A sedan pulls up to the front door.
Two men in Dress Blues.

---

[1] Whipple trees are used in tension to distribute forces from a point load to the traces of draught animals (the traces are the chains or straps on each side of the harness, on which the animal pulls.)

Semper Fi

I sew silence
into the weave of timeless stretch knit
before placing drops of artificial tears into each eye
letting the excess run down both cheeks
as if the disillusionments never happened.

I sew silence
into the weave of timeless patterns—sounds
creaking Corfam dress shoes in early December snow—
crisp powder—overlooking a frozen Wilson Lake.
Taps
hung low in the breath of survivors
sowed grief as a thready heartbeat among the living.

Just Stories

The humility of nondescript panning, rattling bones,
shaking sand from car mats during mud season, fluttering poppy petals,
apple or cherry blossoms
petals without sound float to the bottom of the world. I Ching petals
patterns on new grass. No sound is loud.
The cat brings countless mice to the door.
The deer feed in the backyard meadow.
The front lawn does not get mowed or the truck fixed.
I'm tired of packaged chocolate-covered cherry lies
and the lack of courage to die or live.

Some stories have too much anger, hatred, and shame
to ever be more than fantasy. What can you sell for money?
Market yourself? Prostitute yourself?
Honesty is more than open indulgence.
Honesty, perhaps, is what might be close
to what probably happened
as best as you can recall, depending, of course,
on the person you are telling the story to at that moment.
At that moment a man feared dying alone
so a story was told of a relationship with money, the promise
of justification and glorified hustle.
In another moment, another story was performed.
A story about frustration and the fear of loss
because finally, the protagonist had destroyed
the person and love they desired most.
Their favorite scene was their own hands around their wife's throat
and smashing her head into the hot water tank [a struggle for center stage]
ensued just before she broke two of his ribs and his grip. The protagonist
screamed irrelevantly, "It's none of your fucking business!"

And, of course, it wasn't any of the wife's business,
after all, it was the protagonist's performance and
his fear of love was greater than his fear of loss.

Another classic story
is sung to large drums and the electronic toggle clicks
of police cruisers along desolate Pennsylvania highway ridges at 4a.m.
This Autumnal cantos begins with a funeral ballad in the wind blessed
cornfields of Maryland and the harmonic quietude of respect and honor.
The melodic passage indeed crescendos when a deer
slips back into real time via the radiator and windshield of a Subaru
only to flip one last time through the crack in the predawn sky.
The story sings of a miracle. The female character driving
does not swerve
avoiding the drone of eighteen wheels to her immediate left
and trebled ledges to her immediate right. [Here
is where I confuse the protagonist and antagonist with CODA,]
but, there is a man, if I remember correctly, the husband,
of the female character, I believe, whose trepidation of the dead
whistled as anger through the rattail cord of a payphone
at a 24-hour truck stop in some PA mining town. "It serves you right!
Don't expect me to come and get you and DON'T call me at work!"
[Male character slams phone receiver here] There are two four-beat
measures of silence followed by a repeat the next day
when the female character returns to work where her boss
administers a counseling memo for not following proper
HeadStart company procedure and failing
to call her supervisor at home but instead
called her office at 8a.m. during work hours. Both epic and ghost story,
it continues as a chorus or bardic tale of death and rebirth via
the chromatic scale of subversive prejudices
and the tremolos of malice.
I am telling a story, at this moment,

about people acting like people acting in love
and the innumerable innuendos and windows of opportunities
that the innumerable characters
skillfully imparted into my dreams, visions, aspirations,
in forms of devout jealousy, enlightened manipulation,
high-spirited exploitation. It is an expendable moment
an expendable life, like a disposable lighter or paper cup
a moment captured by the attitudes of human attrition and
cannibalism, instant hedonism, digitized self-sacrifice, and dedication
for the wrong reasons to the wrong people acting out why
it is they feel they don't deserve to be loved and the justifications
continue to vibrate along the spine—a shakedown of coins and shells
upon a board or plate serving up one's mistakes, missed chances,
limited options reflecting age, illness, and isolation.
This is a self-imposed moment of wayward needs never really met
like never really touching a cherry blossom
but a mouth, watering for its fragile skin-like fragrance
like the story of a lover feeding touch
to caged bears through a PVC tube at Animal Land
and just the threat of a hand placing treats in the telescopic sluice
solicits the well-conditioned bears to perform to stop to listen
for the trickling arrival of promise
a freefall from cruelty to concrete
like a rainstick that brings no water just thirst.

the final round

i load my gatling mouth with words
i sport ammo belts of documentation, certification
and identification criteria
        pyres of brass shells gather 'round my feet
commemorative paraphernalia
strung together as a story wampum

sand creek
french campaigns
british campaigns
alcatraz, wounded knee I and II, bloody pond, norridgewock,
vietnam, tora bora, panama, mogadishu, mosul, baghdad,
standing rock—too many, too many to call out

it is hunting season still
and remnants of ejaculated rounds
are scattered among five-hundred-year-old reindeer moss
cartridges of shot gun history
pumped into our children

you want to see protection?

        eagle bone whistles
thunderbirds
of thee i sing

Zophos

a balsam scent sounds its way as a melodic waft
between drone, beat, and grace

the escalator
a rhythmic taiko cadence
into industrial transport dungeons
conveys resigned travelers to a cavernous
Hadean blackhole—

Avant-garde ravens shimmer a gun-blue glint
dive and peck bones clean
even Hell Dogs, guardians of portals, nigh of blessings,
fear the ravens glare and clave-clicking-throat singing

undertones
a zephyr of strings played from speakers recessed in ceiling tiles
cursed distortion never sounding clean enough

don't look back
don't look back

Pods

I don't feel like dancing in my plum body ripe with age
I cut my fingernails to the quick dreaming of my guitar
and singing of warmth that does not come.
I dream of wolves and whales and black and white Orca—
memories breach from cold, salted depths.

The smell of mouse piss dampness
warps paper with waves of barometric pressures
and metered intonations of the unseen.

There is no space in space
or baffles to steady the waves, to nullify the rolling heave
and muffled slosh of discovery
that the woodstove is hot and fire and water are dynamic.
Wood burns with the smell of fall and winter,
cast iron, Agateware, and the transparency of seasons and snow
where it hadn't ought to be at this time
where it hadn't ought to be.

The Boneman

"Always pay the Boneman" Poppa said, pointing his finger
straight up to somewhere unknown
emphasizing with his Hungarian accent
looking at Jerrod who laughed— sort of.
Jerrod was curious about Poppa's stories and sayings
he pulled from the mental margins and white space
of his favorite novels.

I was pensive, leaning on my hand— my neck and chin
contoured the back ridge of the grapevine settee. It was
the manner that Poppa's lips tightened after saying
"always pay the Boneman" that didn't fit with Jerrod's grin.
Jerrod must have known this because he covered his throat too.
It was a way of swallowing our wonder.

      Whose bones did the Boneman have?
      Or maybe he fixed broken bones?
      Why did he have to be paid? With what and how much?

I followed Poppa's jowl to his buttoned collar
and the curious spiral patterns of his loosely knotted tie.
When Momma died last year, Poppa put food out for the night
he said. At the cemetery he stood dabbing his forehead
with the white handkerchief from his suit jacket breast pocket.
He spoke some language, homeland, he said, don't tell your father,
he said, and he sprinkled water and something like cornmeal.
Momma's way is paid, he said, as Jerrod and I scooted
across the front seat of the Plymouth with the steel dashboard
covered with pollen dust because Momma hadn't cleaned it.

Momma's forehead always sweat
in the summer kitchen when she made dumplings,
goulash, potato patties, sourdough breads, and
special secret nut cookies. She had huge hips
like Mr. Polenski's retired milk wagon horse.
Her apron ties remained amazingly still
even when she stirred five-hundred times the secret cookie dough.
Only her hips propelled the wooden spoon.

I miss Momma. So does Poppa, I know
not just because he tells Jerrod and me
but I hear Poppa talking to Momma
when he sits alone on the grapevine settee, no Momma,
just butterflies and catkins still floating in with late summer
early autumn. "Zsuska, my Zsuska, who will sing for me?
Who will pay my way?" Poppa pleads to the cooling air
and cold grass calling Momma by her name.

Poppa showed Jerrod and me pictures of Momma,
his Zsuska, when she was just twenty. Her hair was still thick
like the pony manes at the carnival, dark and a little curly
when the weather got humid. She wore a burnt orange kerchief.
When Poppa tells stories about meeting Momma
the fingers on his right hand reach up under his left sleeve—
he rubs blue numbers, "Your Momma and Poppa
we only had each other" his voice far away,
he would sing in a different language
about camps, he said, that Jerrod and me should never have to know.

Poppa would close his eyes, lean back in the grapevine settee
it bent and creaked as his voice
unraveled a lament like new violin strings

and his sorrow hammered heaven like a dulcimer
waiting to dance with the wind around the base of shade trees
at crossroads and my fingers traced the spirals on his tie
remembering Momma's thick hands and white teeth

I will sing for you, Poppa,
I will sing

Liberty

In an unfinished pine box,
there's a jumble of coins strung as charms on a bracelet.

It is the Mercury dime that draws me in
1942—a clandestine wing on the left side of his helmeted head.

On the coin's backside
my thumb brailles the chopped log forcing
a new growth of leaves.

There is a pressed, damp cold in this room. I hold these coins
as the fire snaps while outside
the rain pours steady. A disconnect
between rain, fire, wooden box, and metal coins—
the fluorescent ballast hums—drones among us
as we work steady and I wonder
about the person who wore this bracelet of charmed Mercury
while dancing, perhaps, on plush oriental carpets
their toes squish between brushed fibers of history,
while, perhaps, their hands and arms snaked
into sinewing undulations as a story, a message, counting beats
with each click of bone joint and vertebral uprising into vapors
of the promiscuous possibility of toes rat-tat-tapping
and we are left
in a slipstream of chance.

Why I Don't Meditate

they said, "close your eyes" "relax" "let your mind see"
roads, I see roads, keep my head down, don't look left don't look right.
narrow, dirt roads, summer mountain meadow roads where there are
goat paths, where the faeries live, or so the locals say,
I see roads lined with tamarack, yellow stone pine, fine sand dusty roads
that ruin camera lenses and jam automatic weapons.
I see white sand beaches that are not alpine and they take me
to New Mexico, White Sands, Alamogordo, Three Rivers, St. John,
North West Scotland, there is warmth
and I travel through Guantanamo, Siboney, (Castro's favorite)
and there in Santiago on the steps at the plaza, the men play dominos
when the women aren't around
or revolutions aren't being waged
or eyes gouged
no retina scrapes clean—

Montgomery, Alabama
I'm pumpin' gas 'round midnight
with the ghosts still blowin' down Rosa Parks Boulevard.

Snake Canyon

I am a simple bridge
connecting one side of the door with the other

silent minimalist design employing brute physics, geometry and guts
a condescending gravity of statements, I am, getting to the bottom of it—

staggering heights of youth, jumping is an interruption
for a moment, a trestled life exposed

I am a simple bridge
straight, direct, sublime with risk

a lanyard of architecture
to traverse the craggy gorge of indifference and prejudice—linearity

freefall—a slow lapse of wind rushes my ears—I was raped—
confessions in the wilderness of naiveté

Bloom

I am the black wisp of hair the wind
curves around your moon jaw
full geisha lips accent red.

Your forehead drips wisteria.

It is summer
the plum pigments painted like stains of bruises on your eyelids
the corners sharp

Deep in repose
your eyes hold windows of recollections flash photographer embedded
in the center of your soul that they did not steal.
You stole them with the effervescence of casual grace
as wind found the few rebellious strands of hair: Shinto

flower vessels float
waves grace
blossom

Waiting for Color

if only her lips curved upward as
an early evening cereus fresh with bloom.

a striking stem and blossom draped languidly
around her neck and over
the angular ridge of a child's clavicles.

it is both alpha and omega
with dripping petals stopped like periods
on her undeveloped breasts.

she has no choice but to wait
to open her mouth
to open her womb
to open her night blooming cereus.

Sustenance

a lover is a delicacy
served with mindful preparation
deliberate placement
refreshing garnish

November

The tomato
like a cup of tea
your hands cupped its essence
an offering your hands made
like feeding doves
I was hungry

A Sacred Sharing

Your thumbs I need to loosen my braid
of three strands, to make one blanket
that spreads across my ermine back.
Your thumbs need to touch my shoulders.
I need you to love me this way.

I'll breathe the wind of February over your lips
only to moisten them
with fresh spring tongue.
My thumbs need to touch your shoulders.
You need me to love you this way.

You won't know the difference
between winter and summer pelt
until your thumbs loosen my braid
that spiders as one web covering our skin
South winds will touch our shoulders
and the median of brown hair
that runs from chest to groin
will weave our bellies as Earth to Sky
where warm summer was meant to grow.

Tulip Trees Blossom

northern Magnolias'
pink-flesh-nape-of-slender-sapling-necks
fragrant with soft hair musked cinnamon as fragrant
as the male Cardinal's throated lolly

summer dawn
        we lied in bed
touching truth

Do Shadows Have Shadows?

i continue to sweep the hallways and corridors of a large house
right to left
i am wondering if wounds ever heal
my body is a tangled schematic of sleeplessness and i am still wondering
if i will have to spend the rest of my life
nurturing salted sorrows—why does this dilemma even exist?

my humanness recalls its uncanny tendency
to trust to love to believe
to soar to become to love
to lick my wounds

sometimes
they are the only thing
a lover leaves

The Silver Side

she drips with sterling hearts
some so smooth they felt wet

chain trickled around her neck
between her brown breasts

a locket hung
rising, falling

warm flesh coddled sterling
capillary etchings, concealed empty chambers

learned to live
with its pinhole flaw, the memory

of a farm boy's hand cupping
the locket, the breasts

caressing with the backs of his hands
so not to chafe her skin

he never saw nineteen
never sat before the camera

that was decades ago in november
when the steers are butchered

their hearts slopped in rectangular cake tins
and the jokes...

how the heart twitches after slaughter
how the fool thing

doesn't even know
when it's dead meat

The Reticent Veil

I never had the grief wiped away
with White Eagle feathers or songs sung
or special foods prepared.

It is true that I dreamt you were sick and dying
and I awoke saying, "This can't be true."
But when our Bear Clan brother came and said it was so
the grief appliquéd itself to my heart
as varicose webbing and loss
which I added to all the many losses
that came and went before you
and they all came back at Ceremony
when me and a Dance brother folded the flag
for the last time on the last day that he handed to me
in a shape that brought it all back to twenty years before
standing on the hillside, looking over Wilson Lake
dress blues, rifles, and Corfam dress shoes cracked
the unusually frigid December where a flag was folded
and handed to me in a shape
that equaled the grief of the world
which came and went as concrete and steel crushed as
the bones and dust I wake up chewing
and it all came back
when me and a sister held taught
a Grande Parade of a royal blue silk veil
maintaining reticent tension—
lovers and wives of warriors, sisters of warriors,
mothers of sons who are warriors—
we folded sharp-angled silence with the precision of lock and load
we creased with steady cadence our losses and recognized each other

not letting go
of the fabric the wind claims for a moment
and my words fluttered
"This is not a flag we are folding."

I am dreaming of you

the smell of your skin
the last time I held your hand
the one a shank sliced leaving the ring finger never to straighten
tendons never long enough
slipping life through the eye of a needle
your breath suppressed, and calm
you hover over me,
like a little boy you ask me to come with you, to play ball perhaps,
or shoot arrows at the peacocks in the Bronx Zoo,
"come with me" you say
your face confused.
"No Poppy, you're dead now.
I belong to the living."

Avalanche

I am a train of silence tunneling through circumstance again
witnessing the privileged exclusion—lack of language
presence of language—rumbling songs—
a whistle of cognition, melodic blah blah blah.
Water turns this wheel that grinds the bones of knowing into flour
bleached by statistics to make white bread.
Let rise not once but twice, double the inflation, double the mass.

I am nothing bursting with a 'Phoon song swoop,
a glacial erratic gouge carving
the valley of Saracen souls
into contours of shale, shiest, and crag.

Wind and water share the same language—
their undertones create soaring lifts
carry sprays of Sahara dust
snagged atop caps of stiff glacial ice
a cinnamon of discriminative circumstance.

At what point does humanness become invalid?

I have grown to despise the invisible walls of assumptions
the spring melt of diagnoses, a placement in a box,
a bank account of withdrawals,
a trickle becomes a flood, a pebble...

It is that easy to take across time and seasons
the loosened rumble of lost permafrost lost
time lost trundles
and the force of nature heaves a shiver

Tibetan prayer flags flutter
hung as trim on a balcony
just outside the station.

The Box

It was supposed to last forever—this box you made for me
a testament of love, its grains of oak, velvet, and hope.

There was the trip to Scotland
always loyal to the earth our mother
the lapis earrings—gates of Ur—discovered in Ullapool
and the broad sword—Norse replica—
Had I returned for it hundreds of years later to recover it
like bones, cave bears, ravens of Innis nan Damh
or dig into the white dunes of Achmelvich
all through the lapis doorways of whatnots?

A beaded tube of tiger eye seeing but not far enough
It was supposed to last forever—our marriage

carved, shaped, glued, and stained—
holds tears of god leaking from the sky
down a rivulet of fine chained sterling into this box
that you stamped your hummingbird seal onto—
the seal I helped you design. It was you, I said, your inner strength
or was it mine that you coveted
squeezed into a little coffin
that you handled with love
glued with fear
and gave away like a child.

There Are No Sides Like The Middle

My ears are ringing again
white bars are electronically drawn apart.
I remove all my silver jewelry—the guards
always ask about my empty pockets
I say, "You should see what's in my boot"
as I stand stocking foot there is no laughter

My ears are ringing again like when men
used to smash the sides of my head—
doors open and close for me as long as I know my I.D. number.
Everything is heavy iron, the windows
are blue-green like Grammie's Ball canning jars—
the ones with the rubber seals
that my mother used for ski harnesses.

My ears are ringing again like when I'd fire
my brother's long barrel .357. There was no kick
the way rifles wedge and separate the shoulder's sinews
of ball and socket. It was slo-mo,
bang and back, like good sex,
the way a weapon ought to move.

My ears are ringing—people holler and scream—adrenalized—
banging bars and walls—tin echoes—
I am late for work
students have waited all week for a callout
my ears are ringing again and I keep forgetting
which side I'm on.

Cold Steel

In the foraging moment
human movement is considered.
It was zero degrees at midday.

Sparks fly from the bouncing blade of a passing snowplow
rattling arches of slush and snow into packed bankings—
packed and patted words for safekeeping
'til natural conditions thaw them one syllable at a time.

We will seek and sift through each ice chunk for meaning
like searching for lost limbs, or digits the snowblower flung
to the stars and Aurora Borealis late at night
and we froze with the realization of "too late".
We'll save what we can and wish
we had done things differently.

Matcha

I knew you when the tea was fresh
not yet steeped in bitterness and pale character. Before
springwater boiled and grew tepid as cordial greetings
no longer an exotic flavor taunting taste buds for words of kindness
love and simple acknowledgment.

I knew you when machismo was you and your carelessness
attracted desperate women Jonesin' for sex
because it was the only validation of beauty they could accept.
And when you became bored, your passion cold, I knew you then.

And when you fell in love for real and it threw you into isolation
like shattered cups against floors, walls, doors—I knew you then too.

When I was a child I fell down a flight of stairs.
I carried my treasured, hand-painted tea set—
mauve pussy willows on cups, saucers, and teapot
the size of a hummingbird's nest—
My tailbone jackhammered each solid stair, from my hands
exploded Japanese porcelain, my childhood
shards of innocence, vaporized, all hope
an intermittent rumble of moans.

I saw a little boy in your eyes full of joy and love
throwaway books, pictures, gifts
like the boy who knew he had lied,
stole, killed, survived, knew himself
to be bad, unforgiving, undeserving.
Shame and guilt make a bitter brew
I knew you then too.

129

Tea.
I held you
when you brought flavor, comfort, warmth.

How much guilt?

Gold highlights in her hair beckon like the heart of Buddha.
A star—ancestral—pierced with suffering bled into a living tree
our only hope to ascend—go home—enter into, onto, a path of service.

The gold highlights flicker as tongues of flame as eyes in darkness
refract a search light bent on scanning for validation
that someone, something, is out "there" a mirror of intent and action
taking chances
only to confirm, the human ogre, the tempestic predator, lacks soul.

Why do we continue
to search
the hearts
to bring home
our kind?

Leave no soldier behind

How long

do we search?

As long as it takes.

The Train I Call the Kosovo

I am riding the train in-between cars with a couple of Serbs.
We did not pay for first-class tickets

How do I recognize the old man wearing a rumpled, wide lapel
polyester powder blue suit?
He recognizes me too and in a language of his own he tells
the younger travel mate from Belgrade, the translator,
to turn my suitcase sideways so I can sit.

"No money, no woman" the only English he speaks
and offered me a 1000 Francs.
I laugh he laughs my answer is no.

He straddles a toddler's first bike and steals a moment
when the translator leaves to take a piss
and in quick fragments like sudden brushstrokes with clear eyes he draws
a picture—words of a woman he's been with for two years,
and souls he speaks of like white accents in a mural
he points to with his chin to the translator
now sitting on the narrow stairs to the upper level first class.

The man from Belgrade relays the color of language and curiosity
with the money man watching closely the translation,
"Have you traveled much? He notice that you relaxed. You live?"
I respond to the money man, "Yes. I live."

And like a trance of wind that wraps the head as a turban
his hands of rough knuckles wrapped his head in cantos he moaned
"Kosovo. Kosovo. The Americans—the bombs the bombs—no sleep."
The translator says "no, no speak about that."

132

My arrogance and pride are calm
because somewhere in the knowing is a cliché worth repeating.
All the money in the world cannot buy my soul.
Some days, I wish it could.

Teal Blue Doors

Next year at this time
I will walk up these steps through grottos and wisteria and
knock on this teal-blue door that faces the coming and going
of sailors, fishermen, tides pulling sunsets
between the bay's standing stones that hold
broken ships, buoys, and caves
that accent serpentine meanderings—
the longest part of the journey home
is a blue door waiting to open.

A toothless Gramma smiles, opens her arms. A crackling hearth
releases the smell of warm cast iron and tea.
"Come in and sit" she'll say.
"Tell me your story" she'll say
while steamed tea is poured and buttered island biscuits
are offered with goat cheese, olives, and garlic,
to bring healing after weeks at sea.
If she has marinated fish she will offer that too,
but never ask for anything.

Travelers know what a tourist may not,
that in the backroom
she burns candles made from fat and prays
for all voyageurs.
All journeys
begin and end this way.

Along the Shore—Five Miles

The hollow tapping of ice thumps against the rock shoreline.
It is a hulled January of cold and better times—
a wintered vessel of black water lapping out of fog and snow squall
makes my teeth ache—longing for sweetness.

We have all been here before
along the ridge of Tongue Mountain Range
Kanien'kehá:ka and the Abenaki—a Nor'east vengeance.

The Arctic wind makes my bones ache
the way breath blows through the hollow of wood
a throbbing melody in A flat minor.

In Between

A photo album of life and times—
stuttering, stopping—
false starts, rough endings—

And yet here in this space of humanness
in black and white archaic pixels—before pixels' grayscale—
we are too familiar, too close, to life's tragedies and injustice
covered by vellumous joy.

What kind of animal are we
that does not recognize
we are all related?

The Boy in the Water —witness

The Boy—
like water tumbling to a puddled stop for the wind to quiver its surface—
his brown hand extended across the tops of many hands
to a man he had never met
who received with palm turned sunward
toward the source—Allalin—the milk of many
and this hand that received across the valley of differences
recognized the water in the water—

I heard the echo—I heard the whisper called a gesture—
"Same, Same" our skin the same color
and I recalled a moment

a Lakota man in Vietnam[2]
tightened his grip on an M-16
a Gramma runs from a hut and pleads,
"Same, Same" her hand touching his.

---

[2] **Warriors** a film documenting Native American Vietnam Veterans.
http://redeyevideo.org/Warriors.html

Impressive Education: Mrs. F. the librarian

So many stories about differences because we were different.
Our family had stories that everyone in town knew
and whispered. We had dark people
in our family. Our first language was not English.

The school librarian knew we were different.
I held a thick book—can't recall the name or author—
it was about a Catholic priest and nuns
taking WWII Jewish children over an Alpine pass
Italy to Switzerland—Saas-Grund, Saas-Fee—
Children that didn't know
why they were hunted, tortured, shot, alone.
With my two hands I gripped that book
reluctantly presented it to Mrs. F.
into her translucent hands boney, spotted with age
her pasty skin and pinched sharp nose—she smelled like mothballs.

She tugged the book from my hands
using her closed fingered knife-hands
to wipe it off where I had touched.
"You're not intelligent enough to read this book."
Her statement made, she turned on her skinny ankles
her heels clicking into the darkness
of book stacks and metal shelves.

I told my oldest sister that night.
The next day she brought me the book.
I imagined my 4-foot 10-inch sister, her darkness,
French accent, her black fire opal eyes,

her hand sliding the book across the checkout counter.

I read the book and returned it
just to let Mrs. F. know
that silence does not mean ignorance.

I write this poem sitting at the base camp in Saas-Fee sipping espresso
taking a break from doctoral studies
having hiked the passes
with survivors of the mountain guides from WWII.

Oh yes, Mrs. F., I understood then
as I understand now
prejudice is nondiscriminatory.

Mediterranean Blues

The baby is a pool toy washed up by the surf.
A red, yellow, blue beachball baby—
half deflated, face down, the inevitable tide nuzzles,
teases the suppleness of thick black toddler hair—
rocks its ebb and flow there in wet sand of sodden hope.

It's like wind, perhaps, or a mother's breath that puffs
a stinging insect away or the quick pulse of fingertips
that brush away sticky crumbs from a morning shirt
from breakfasts past—

Family—and a promise of a future—
like any family on any beach plucking shells
from squawking gulls—

Where are we in this violent eddy of riptides and terror?

Who are we as humans awash with technology and fanaticism?

We are adrift

We are adrift

Grace

Tea with the Gods comes from sweat, salt, peace
and careful placement of foot in front of foot.
turquoise sky—sharp January arctic blasts
prism the midday sun into a corona of color.

There is silence—the silence of Chickadees, Nuthatches,
 muted thuds of Downies and Hairies pecking punked wood.
There is the silence of micro-spikes on snow and terraced ice steps
narrow trail, rhythmic crunch, and fluttered fall of dry Beech leaves.

There is the pace, counting steps—
deer have eaten bead-sized Alder buds
the snow loosens with depth—a frozen type of sand. Journey on
the summit breeches from the grip of glacial erratics—

In winter Birch offers chaga. Summit Fir has grown tall.
Snow not blown from the ice crust holds the story of Deer,
Rabbit, tail tracks made from Fisher and Fox.
Hunting strategies of Coyote are woven by the braided tracks of three
braided among Beech, Oak, and Maple and the slender pillars creak
with twisted stress from wind—brittle from sap sucking subzero cold.

Gazing across the valley, across the Sacandaga, across the surface
of Fir Ghillie-hidden homes—the vaporous breath of only one woodstove
wicks up river moisture, rises up
from my black, honeyed tea
silence of the Wind

drinking the self
drinking the Universe

It Is Not A Swiss Train

It is a train whose tracks I drove by for fifteen years
imagining a train slow-snaking its undulation along the Hudson
like the riverwater itself emerging from ice-jams at 30 below 0 eeking
towards revelations
I hum a Chris Smither's tune, mouth the words dyskinetically
"I am not the passenger, I am the ride."

An exotic ride
through railing marriages, raising two sons, grad school fulltime
while working three and four jobs. It felt good
to ride along 418 up through Thurman Station
where the Schroon dumps into the Hudson
where Teddy Roosevelt made his connection
via guides, reeling stagecoaches,
and avalanched into history—McKinley was dead.

Like the iron rails laid by force, dedication, and sacrifice, I survived
the blowdowns, and rockslides, political misconceptions, depressions
of economic catastrophes—like this train
these tracks carry through floodplains and Honeysuckle gone wild
I too am the wind of the sharp piercing kind rain threatens to freeze
the way an uncapped pen threatens to write
parted lips threaten to speak.

A slow train
is a lullaby hushed by blossomed Red Sumac
cradling the broken tarmac that runs
parallel with the rail-bed of blueberries and white pine—
a small boy to father says, "But there's a window in my way."

Mumma the Volcano

I could growl for lifetimes
opening my mouths
as gateways
to Heaven and Earth

I am
the Red River

My Mother's Tree

A picture frame—four corners to the world—filigree.
Edessa, I see you sitting in your tree.
I know you climbed there yourself.
My fingers run along the beaded edge of solder droplets,
tiny pinhead drops of silver, or mercury or the hot corn syrup
and lemon pudding you made from scratch
that balled up in cold water when it was done.

You had amazing focus when you baked
and allowed us kids to play barefoot in January
because the old Glenwood Parlor stove in the basement
kept the floors warm. You were as expansive
as the illusory curves of this picture frame my fingertips fondle
counting the corners while murmuring with thumb and forefinger
ticking your lead crystal rosary
the one you kept in the metal pouch of Italian fish scale silver.

It's this kind of magic that beautiful women sitting in trees,
back against the trunk, legs casually crossed at the ankles
extending down the branch, carry,
and apply to their hardships.
You could not keep me out of trees either
even after falling, even after living in the White Pine like Fisher Cat.

Unseen air aspects spirit us to treetops as breath, push us
from trees to kitchens to domesticity to anger to violence to wisps
of consciousness, turbulent emotions:
It was not o.k. to be beaten.
It was not o.k. to be raped.
It was not o.k. to give your soul

to a man your naïveté created as your savior
who betrayed you for being human
with his piloting good looks that honeyed you down from your tree.

It is a different kind of love
that baked ten—twenty loaves of bread at a time
made fresh donuts at 5a.m., enough turkey to feed forty
two-hundred-plus quarts of canned string beans,
pickles, relish, tomato sauce, beet greens—

You forged your way to the Earth
your feet always bare in summer.
How they longed to take flight.

Northwest Highlands

I don't know how to make the sky pink as cotton candy.

Squint my eyes? Become the mountain crags,
a creek of stones rolling to the Loch or ocean or both?
All water flows to the ocean—
ships—
there is food, fish, trapped in the pools of water
and we hopscotched from stone to stone a gulfstream
of a child's game for us but the shadows knew different,
knew a time when survival was not a game.

Shadows touch the fish.
I see now how lonely a shadow could get. They whisper
about vessels and war. I feel the weight of oak in my heart creak,
ease to and fro, a pilgrimage—constant journey,
constant, I tell you, constant pink awash the mountains,
Dolomite outcrops, water, heather, time, space, and snow
on domed peaks—take refuge in the caves
as a recluse, crab, or prawn walking backwards into the pores
of mountains sounding back that we must move forward

As a smear of pink across tree lines black with borders of possibilities
across these pages
of childhood losses, secret places, cellophane transparencies,
between one life and the next.

Steelies

I'm not afraid.
I persevere through rhythmic waves of hardship and crests
of foam-salted success. Red-Tailed Hawks drift and lift
between March winds, thawing sun melts snow.

Mud means new marbles for playing,
plucking, thumb popping, in graveled muck alive with Earth's waters.
Another winter we survived.
The sap runs as snow secedes
as creatures awake. We have survived, I tell you
as clouds disperse as stars emit as planets converge
as tree-snapping horror falls in the forest, we have survived.

I give you new reasons to jump rope double-dutch
with a kind of darkness that
procreates jealous whispers that
we have survived and stuffed
our lessons into tin lunch boxes, in pouches
and plastic baggies we carry Cat's Eyes,
Bumblebees, Biggies, Puries to schoolyards,
playgrounds, parking lots, abandoned countries—

The stakes are high
and we keep our Steelies hidden from foot stompin' bullies
keep them in our front pockets accessible to our best throwing hand
our secret power ready to thumb pop and smash the glass eyes
ready to sling like stones that took down Goliath.
We have survived,
I tell you,
survived.

Abbera Ka Dabbera

Then
there was enough innocence to find
the masses staggering punch drunk on hope
fantasy and hocus pocus. There were clowns
and tricksters that lead us through the shit
while visualizing cool moss under fir trees
where even wind clamors to go.
Then
like spigots jammed open
torrential buckets of rain pounded the earth
faucets closed, the sun came out, and we saw
the truth drying between our childish toes.
What matters, then, became the realization
that recess was over and the notorious taskmaster of maturity
reigned in our expansive visions, our play, our singing.

There is more in the doing as Elders pass
and we became the ones watching the play.
        Did we take care of our Elders? Did the Elders
          watch to see which child considered the other?

What matters, then, is how we drank the water that youth did not need.
In this dangling fruit that passes quietly to seed
there is not consumption, assumption, or spoil—
what matters, is where do the seeds fall
             where do they take root?

At the Barker Place around dismantled stone foundations
and mysteriously covered wells staggered
between bear eating apples

off the ground around the base
of Cortlands, Martha Washingtons, and Northern Spies—
Honeybees zigzagged the deer standing on hindlegs
reaching through extended necks and narrow tongues
for the prized apples in high branches—
autumn fruit that black bears could not shake loose.

In the poetry of progress
the historical line of fancy and memory,
even the scythe of time cannot cut.

The Darkest Spot Is Light

I never knew where Raven lived
except perhaps at a roadside diner

Never thought Raven needed nests or
could coo lower than Mourning Doves

could roll the ocean in his throat more slowly
than Heron flapped their wings

Raven's hypnotic language
are shadows that never leave

any who dare listen to Raven's empty baskets of wind
are mesmerized—this is how

Raven gives or takes dreams
listen to the rolling drumbeat in my throat

I dare to touch you
I want my dream back

Flashpoint

Under a full moon, Chicago sprawls.
Its sodium streetlights spill like orange Fanta
July Fourth effervescence explode
looking down upon the pool of neighborhoods, blocks, and barrios
the wingtip lights of this small jet flash—
rendered irrelevant—not bright enough.

white sound fizz of the engines and laminar flow
a midi four-track of sounds to the retinal bursts of silent fireworks
the layer of complexities: perhaps here one could discuss race riots
or the irony of who really created the Constitution
perhaps a simple taste is all that is necessary to both emphasize
and appreciate the depth of implications
that no more effervescence means
flat existence—the celebration ends
long before light of day—

Road to the Stars

I trust the light of day rising up from behind the two mountains
at my front door. I trust the East Wind
that blows up the hill and over the lodge. I trust
the fire that burns, the snap of wood catching,
the smell of hot stones in soft darkness,
red or white with heat and the sound
of flat cedar searing into smoke.

I trust the delicacy of sweetgrass
melting into fragrance—into beauty, steam, and breath
the water poured over rocks
like starlight over the meadow that is my backyard
pouring over my flesh, cascading into my body
my sweat, I trust my sweat the release
of resistance, the power
of simply letting go of the weight of human emotions.

I trust the honesty
and revelation in the rapturous black line in the sky
water singing into wind or ocean waves
this cadence of life in this womb of all things
we are everything and nothing.

I see my mother in the Milky Way
she reminds me of the last time I was "put out" in a pit of darkness
it was over a hundred degrees. I wrapped myself in a quilt
shivered with cold—there is no escaping—she reminds me
we were born this way.

We were born this way.

IV

Swimming in the Eagle's Eye

When I was a small child I would sit in the woods
on an island much like this one in the postcard with Birch
and Hemlocks, White Cedar scattered in the background
of a gestational mound of earth—a kind island.

There was a pond that no one seemed to know about
but me, of course, and I went there often.
The mosquitoes didn't bother me—
I was accustomed to their penetration
and nuisance from fishing.

The pond was endless depth calm:
"Don't look into the eyes of the Wakinayan!"
"Don't make eye contact with the Heyoka!"
That's what Uncle always warned.

I would stare at that pond for what seemed like hours
sometimes it was. I watched
water skippers and reflections of backward worlds,
turned-upside-down worlds and the point
at which they became right side up.
A bowtie of angled realities.

An eye of the earth, the pond,
an ancient eye of an elephant, or octopus,
dark with depth that tunneled into blackness—the void
of falling dreams into turbofans of wind rushing in your ears
and you wake up someplace else.

I had been through this pond before.

154

I recognized something
in this Eagle's eye
this everything and
nothing
striking calm.

When the Glacier is Gone

It is not a door at all
but a place by the white birch
a bench welcoming as
the breath of fog, the breath of morning.

I walk there
holding memories like orange peels
in crumpled brown paper lunch bags.
I recall the smells of blood oranges in Italy, fresh glacial melt
frigid with the milk of life and hot
with Andalusian whispers of Saracen movement
the djinn of Sahara windblown across Alpine nipples
turned iron oxide red from dust and blood of millennia.

An Ash tree quivers in the background—
jettisoned to the outer reaches of historical error,
present and waiting for a sunrise,
a crack between worlds between the shrinking crevices
worn deep from spring melt to fill soulless buckets with substance.

There is peace by the sculpted Juniper,
Bishop's Weed, Purple Cone Flower, Bee Balm—
tall Irises skinny from stretching upward—
fingerlike tendrils and nerves grasping for gods
memories, life, reason.

My mother taught me how to climb trees.
My favorite photo of her sits at my bedside.
She is young, her legs follow
the contour of a large, extending tree limb—

She is laughing and her arms drape—a lioness in the Ash of life.

It is the morning fog of sunrise
the receding tide of dew
that washes away historical clutter
reveals a story, a fossil, a coin.

Between Lovers and Light

I thought
I had seen the last of your shadow
and the emotions that your presence
evokes from me
as though
my soul were an extraction
of mints and yarrow.

And there you were
one day,
dangling in my heart, you,
the last autumn leaf, red,
and trembling from the kisses of breath
and the not so subtle convincing
that it's time for you to go.

And yet,
perhaps, it is me that holds tight
to the brittle contradictions of pensive hesitation
of being separate and inseparable.

Oh, my branching soul prays
with every pulse of touch
my hands can give
for you to stay.

I thought
I had seen the last of your shadow.
My mistake.

The Smell of Blood

there is old plum blood clumped like grapes becoming raisins
dry and cracked on the edges, crystallizing like nano birdshot.

there is fresh blood vibrant as lips wearing lipstick
for the first time red with life and air
and knowing nothing but that moment in the gasping for more.

there is the in-between blood that grows sticky with flies
like fruit juice spilt on clean linoleum that no one wants to talk about

as it has already been spilt and cleaning up the mess implies our guilt
so we sip quietly with downcast eyes onto tabletops in outdoor cafes

or our mother's favorite butcherblock and we pray
that dogs enter soon to lick up taboos now sticky with truth.

there is the pink frothy blood that effervesces into mist
alive with the last Kiai—last words, last breath, last action,
beyond form and recognition.

there is the blood we suck from a papercut, bright as words
we sliced with time. never
is blood alone but mingled with bitter gall, and bile, or the rank of gut
and brains.

there is the blood of unborn fetuses in glass vacuums
and plastic measuring cups in deep sinks
power-washing the rot of vaginal infections
and there is the blood of life tainted with umbilical mater—
amniotic fluids, saline, and protein enhanced with sweat

cannaling through mergences, cavernous, cold, sally port pelvises.

there is the blood of death spattered with the last shit you'll ever take
and no one cares what your last meal was
but you and whoever made it.
Tabasco pizza, chocolate chip cookies melted into blobs from heat
while being shipped from runway to runway,
or sitting in back postal rooms in mail bags.

there is the blood of transfusions, transformations, transportation
into Warferin, Heparin, and morphine drips.

there is the blood of lies
the blood of truth, the blood of consequences, conflicts,
confusion that titrate into the soil and dust of everyday living—
the absence felt
when mowing the lawn
getting the mail
feeding the dog.

there is the blood of abstraction, nightmares, invaders
of songs, stories, horror metered by heart palpitations
tightening of chest and the constant neurotic obsessive unlocking
re-locking of doors, windows— load, fire, reload.
there is the blood of love that dries too quickly into a cacophony of
smells that embrace something someone somewhere describes as life.

Blood,
I smell you on flesh, in bathroom stalls, laundry baskets,
garbage cans, drain traps, band aids in locker rooms,
knee patches stiff with iron.

I smell you on the streets in the lives outside of reasoning.

Throwing Stars

At first, I thought someone was frying peanut butter
but it was you, it was you,
your charred face
brittle on the flight mask.

Dog tags you didn't wear any more than seatbelts
tinkled in the cargo-hold dangling from the mouths of luggage
from which clothing exploded, hung up in the moment,
and wavered like an aftershock from the aftershock
from the vacuum of the generators and their
brazen light cauterized death into dampness and late autumn pines.

Heavy frost in Poland Springs—the water froze
from incidents occurring too close to home
and the five stars arrived and the M-16's arrived and the media arrived
and the body bags arrived but you and your buddies
had already gone, flew the coop.

Like Spanish Moss and old olive oil,
your uncontained rancidness leaked through the evergreens.
I never saw your children
I never saw your wife I never saw your mother and father
but I saw the jerk with the camera and his curiosity snatching
memorabilia. Perhaps he wasn't high tech enough.
Perhaps he didn't realize all sensitive material had been removed
or maybe we were in his backyard, but really,
it was everyone's backyard.

Howard Hughes only drank Poland Springs water, but not that night.
No one drank from the springs that night

you busted out of the sky, a screeching fireball,
a pencil point projectile pop-stabbing through an astronomical poster
you slashed to the Earth, wind-sheared white pine tops,
plowed autumn fields for two miles and burnt.
You were blown out of the vast indifference of space and attitude,
you just didn't make it home fast enough,
just didn't missile under the livewire soon enough.
Most only knew the half of it and the other half couldn't give a shit.
Orion fell. We looked for body parts.

Twenty years later when I'm at the park in Saratoga,
You'd hardly notice that I knew anything.
And if it weren't for my hyper-olfactory,
I would have forgotten you.

I can smell mothballs for miles, jet fuel for days—
sticks to the roof of my mouth sends me anaphylactic—
I can feel the inside tire blow on a tractor-trailer, before I hear it.
A friend had to stop eating meat, can't even be around it,
reminds him of reconnaissance.

And while jammin' once in the park
a drunk fell to the marble ground at the sulfur spring
trying to dance and drum at the same time but did neither.
Words soothed him. In unwavering quiet
he listened to words, to poetry, the only one
who understood, this drunk had nothing to do with you,
but if he had had a mask
it would have looked like yours.

Grist

We meet in this world of grayscale shadows seeking
the curves of jaws, baby-soft flesh
petals of Magnolia's orchid essence—a twist of scent—
my heart races, floodgates open, pound release
like greyhounds like Preakness stampede—explosive water—

The waterwheel at Grampa's old grist mill clattering red oak paddles
strip-search each drop of mill pond recklessly escaping
into Lemon Stream an exodus
of power careening across the dam-harnessed captives—each drop
a tortured witness scooped to bear its strength,
to be exploited
in a Kalic spin of revolution
powered the millstones
from pond calm as sphagnum
calm as suckers fanning in cool shadows
emerge from one primal mess to another

It is you again
still seeking dreams still holding the past,
our shaky bog
our sponge of regret

if i could tell you this

swallows would slice through blue-black thunderheads
like bats from Howe's Cavern or caves in France
or the one in Scotland where I found Raven feathers and bone.

This, I say quietly as the Cardinal sings
in the heavy scented-as-death Honeysuckle
covered with bees and dew
I would say
I miss you
a rumble of grief
a strike of truth
maintain
maintain

Blossom

red-fluted throat
cavernous for your tongue
hummingbird

Moments

The bear awoke standing.
The wolf, an alarm clock,
early—the day of coffee and sun and cardinals and hawks
and trusting the intuitive.

Tea Tree oil around the hairline, motorcycles packing the road
packing the car, packing the air with brightness
leaving the phone in the car and off.

The air is sweet with sounds of nuthatches, wrens, phoebes, and robins
chipmunks and the wind's subversive breath of life seeped between
fir boughs, goosefoot maple, and ash.

The sun—always dappling—the undergrowth
and the quiet pond not yet full of August algae and waterlilies.

After a while

The haul itself offers a rhythm of percussive bumps and ruts
a washboard of life, metal gray, like the wet memories
of washing bird's eye diapers on the creek shore
because you wanted to experience the hardships
of living off-grid goin' granola.
It was the antithesis of structure.

Sun, moon, sun, moon—and after a while, I realized,
that we could never be permanent
I recall my fascination
with those early '60s paddleball toys
we bought at Hodgkin's General Store
right beside the four-pack candy Pall Malls
real penny candy, the meat counter just steps away from the post office
you could not circumvent the practical aisle
of hunting boots, ice-fishing gear and plaid wool jackets
hung in the store front windows
behind brittle orange cellophane.
Never did we think these things would vanish.

After a while
any hardship only fuels the Rough Rider
keepin' clean is a vulnerable exception and I understand
why Mumma always wore her WWII pearls
like a moon phase calendar
gracing her tie rod clavicles.

on my way home

from crystal white sands and boiling storm waves—
early afternoon—the quiet hums with the engine's white noise
an idle of background basso continuo
peppered staccato of backup beeps—rhythmic shrills

muffled thuds of luggage are rubricked into the jet's cargo hold
the blast of colorful luggage snapped into place
becoming the secured scales of a dragon's belly,
slowly the beast rolls, slowly,
the beast eases into liftoff.

it's the part i like best
the part where thrust tears away from g-force
my body left heavy on the tarmac
and for a moment i remember floating
above the sediment above
the body weight of a rapist above
the weight of casket flags above—
above it all

Spiral

I am the bone of bear skull
I am the vertebrae emerging from the base of a cavernous vessel
howling into the dangling undulation called a spine
my soul is the dry marrow used for gardens
in cautious amounts— the power to grow—
the power to kill

I am the bones of all worlds
I walk through gates, doors, caves, streets of revelations,
on the steps of blood and revolutions, in churches, basilicas,
fields burning the dead, birthing rooms and christenings
I am the breathy whispers that thread your hair—
I am the absence in your heart—
The dead will always dance you.

Serf

It is a recurring dream—
I keep walking into the ocean.
The sun is hot and melts away the grime of stress,
double-crosses, burdens. I wear white gauze
the frayed hem flutters, a salted breeze skittered perpendicular wakes
across white sand.

I throw myself
into an open embrace
of crisp sun-starched linens hung in Cuban courtyards
and march into the ocean.

Freedom
is the hair swirling about the corners
of a mouth full of laughter.

Peace
to resolve in a fully present body—
my tour of duty.
Duty.

Día de Muertos: Remember Who Feeds You

(inspired by Diego Rivera's *Sunday Dream at Alameda Park* 1947.)

In her chiseled skull she held elegance. Isabella.
Her boa feathers fanned out like vertebral wingtips. Her hat
a magnificent statement with ostrich plumes and foxglove blossoms
further dignified this queenly moth's fine bone fingers curved
as a chilling muff around the arm of her living escort—a remaining
husband, son or lover, perhaps.
She holds the hand of a young boy, the only other one smiling
in this familial portrait. He holds her folded umbrella
its vulture head handle counterbalance
to the snake escaping from his pocket.

A crowd. A clustered soiree of gabardine waistcoats
a processional of black derbies and flannels
ensconced solemnity accompanied Isabella like a shadowy aura
of being forgotten or as a calculation to be ignored
like a stolen hat thrown into a crushed box
pulled from the garbage with a scrap of holiday paper stuck obtrusively
to the collapsed corner—no card, no nametag just an
"Oh, here take this" the accidental gift just before midnight.

When Isabella lived, she labored and broke free of chains—
every link an expectation—Isabella dedicated every breath
to birthing, love, meals, and patience. She only knew
how to live and carried burdens in her keen eyes and silent mouth
even then you could see the knife edge of her cheek bones glint
across the oceans of a disciplined jaw she kept closed.

171

The truth shall free you from the solidity of darkness,
the checkerboard of deceit and the broom of lies
sweeping hair off the floor for someone else to place their feet upon
or changing the sheets for someone else to be held in. In the dustpan
broken promises, thick dreams and grains of words, "You and I,
You and I. It's just You and I."

Isabella paid her dues with requited subjugation
and found power in her well-stacked bones with their generational
rings of integrity, scores of memories, ledgers of emotional debtors.

Isabella still walks amused in her ghostly aftermath and sends a wake
of paranoia throughout her surviving
friends and lovers who fear death and women
who can smell other women
and hear frayed lies in thready voices fabricating excuses,
and scenarios
like an over-washed bath towel with broken strings
getting caught on the unintended door knob, and bed frame

like stuck-in-your-throat-dust-balls jammed into corners
the furnace blows them there, narcissism keeps them there, outside
of accountability and ownership. Isabella
stopped cleaning other people's houses.

In death she walks assured of her original instructions, finds peace
in her place of sisters, women who bury the dead
who stand by the gate
they are the gate, the grotto, the pelvic girdle
of life and death, she paid her dues and waits by the gate
for past escorts, husbands, lovers who fear dying
almost as much
as they fear living.

Pearl

It is all that I have
what have I ever lost by dying? Raindrops
light on the autumn pond, appear as the mouths of trout, bass, or
minnows feeding on the delicacies of late black flies and mosquitoes.
The bullfrog throats a bass to the upper-registered chickadees
and tenor jays punctuated by downies and nut hatches'
percussive picking clean the fir and balsam.

A cacophony, really, entwined with woodsmoke, sirens
and long-haul trucks mitigating the valleys these measured sounds
skid across the glassed pond as a prow slicing current
or a paddle's cutting edge.

A moment is an opportunity to gather senses
to realize myself as something greater
than the solo existence
of my snotty nosed sore back cleaning stovepipes
stacking cords upon cords
of stiff bodied wood

greater than a perceived condition that never really held true
like a pond shivering ripples of wind
just when we think we can step through.

My grandmother's name was Alice, Alice Pearl. Did you know
that pearls are kept clean by peeling their layers of calcification,
to expose the fresh opalescence
the gleam and shine of ligament milky white?
Each layer removed by the scraping of the moon of all nights
the layers of all love, revealing

the horrific depth of all living
down to the bone truth—
disappearance
were we really ever here?

Singing Across the River

"Fly, Mumma, fly!" that's what I said
fanning her face with a dance fan made just for her
and this moment. Final phase, we call it—
small druzy salt crystals formed around the creases of her nose.

It was my turn to sit with her.
It was after midnight. She and I had done all our talking.
She would not go to Hell, she said, because she gave the priest
one last chance to forgive her.
She forgave him for refusing to administer her last rites.
"No," I said, "you will go home to the stars."

Early on Mumma and I found a purple pouch
that would be her travel bag. She agreed, she would travel light.
She and Dad, me, my sister, Aunts and brother agreed
that the bag would not ever be removed from her body. We made
a pact that no one, not even Dad, would look inside.
Mumma packed the things she wanted to keep in her heart.

I never looked in her pouch but I know
she took a cassette tape of me singing my own songs.

It is a complex thing
this singing spirit's home.

Tobacco—Sweet like Chocolate

love—like smoke rain prayers
brown thrushes in wooded underbrush
a song so beautiful i can only bear to hear once.

tobacco—sweet like melodic chocolate sprite of bird
i was innocent enough to hear
to be still enough to pause
alone in the fir and balsam a flutter
of whistles and trills i savored on my tongue tip
the recollections of mystery and flavors
like nutted scents of vibratos
the bitter of silent tremolos—
where do the songs come from?

Fire

i eat dirt.
crawl over stones, molten glass, white coals
i tend eternal fires
burn into night sweats—matrix-convoluting-matrix—
until a spark of gesture stirs the past
to which you add twigs of touch and glances of wind.

i'm tired
pray i can hold on long enough
to dry damned tears that streak my face like a dirty windshield
long enough to hold my bloody heart to the lips of gods
who know how to love
and don't blame me
for being human.

Caput Mortuum *opus extremus*

I will die listening to the Brandenburg Concerto
as though nothing
out of the ordinary had occurred.

Strings of adornment will waft through the air like pennants
snapped by a down-draft or brisk up-sweep
or whirl of disintegration of events—evening scores—
notes for the absent.

A life measured by soundless eddies of conflict
ripples of relationships emerge
nostalgic tones and tapped accents
they are dreams scattered betwixt the buoyancy of joyous encounters
on white sand terrains, in rainforests dropping geckos, or
snowmelts awash with frigid minerals swept
into valleys lined with Stone Pine, Linden, and wandering goats.

Throughout these seasons inside of seasons
a geist connects the capillaries of time.

Have some symphony with your dalliance with fate
one last crescendo, if that's what you can call it,
the subtle meter of destiny that wakes no one
whose life became a jingle box tinkling with struggles,
whimsy, survival, passion, children, history—

A sparkling effervescence splashes—
conclusion—acceptance—
sub-Saharan Bullfrogs, dung beetles, brittle bones,
crocuses.

Mish'ala

More emptiness
what does it mean this space with no men, no sun
matrix, caldron, unraveling nebulae—the consciousness of mass
Mata, the Mother, the depth of power potential
the swirl of DNA, a spiral staircase bean-stocking
to the beginning of time?

When the sun came there was a warmth
like the heat of the first menstrual blood flow
a tear from the womb of void begetting
the first drop of ocean.

Is it true?
Is it true that the Great Mystery
is but the womb of the Universe found
uterally in each female being, creature, element
that twists and spins among the gases?

It is my story too
how the nucleic ions splashed across my moist secrets of womb
stirring in the essence of action—the man as flavor—
the herb of vigor, the stem of design—

My story is a poppyseed of delicacy, a peppercorn of truth,
an onion flake of memory—
salt

Holding On

Spring lilt
is the new, lime-green leaves of the Passionfruit plant
sitting in the southeast window.
The green singing gets louder
with each second longer the sun conducts its risings.
It is a tonal buzz, a throat singer's hum, a vibration on a string
from one can to another,
a crackled vibration along phonelines and cables at twenty below zero—
      this hum
is green with life.

There is no dispute in its melodic
movement the color of Spring,
only a break, this January thaw
enough to turn our minds around
a revival, passion just wanting to live
because we don't know any better.

Galilee

It has come to this has it?
Strands of gossamer we weave
us women warriors we fight different
we survive
welcome home
to our sisters ready for change
that wakes us in dreams
throbs in our flesh
like pounding mochi into sweetness—nougats of trauma.

Like us kids in Temple at the summer church on the intervale
we pulled the thick jute rope
our child hands could barely grip as we clung
like braided garlic hoisted and dropped
Oh, Hemingway, ring the bell
that us kids clamped tight, our palms red and roughed
our bodies twisting, feet flapping like live trout
on a Y-branch-bough brought home to Mum
to gut and fry.

A Crescent of Bone

Bleached bones
sharp white
like summer bedsheets stiffened
by starching sun and arid wind

Domes white
with history
pounded alleys sandal trodden
swirled by the eddied circumference of jelabiyas' hem

Coolness resides
in concave steps
hands read the wall as brail
delicate fingertips to the fossilized shells
anemones
there is power in walking
where another civilization has walked

We cannot hide as children
in the shawled stairwell as a cowered creature
while our history annihilates our future

Iron Sight

Moment bright
swim through the eye of an open heart
flashes of life the color of amniotic
as the return of warmth
or song of water or
the thudded sounds of whatever fears
we must emerge from
to get to the next phase of being

Last Ride with Dad

A snow of mimosa petals bleaches the roadside's graveled shoulders
a yellow fragility spreads across the fresh drops of flutter
drops of fragrant moments, a pall of nicotine, age on paper,
of a white dress worn by narrow-waisted women
crystallized in silvered tintypes or brownie prints and Polaroids.

It is mid-June in west central Maine
and even the lilacs are slow to release their lavender petals,
but they do.
There is surrender
to emotions and time and memory and the unknown
we can hope for terrain traveled
threads
from continent to continent
a current stream of movement
from life event to life event.

the dead are not dead

the grasses weep.
thirty years ago, I looked across the valley of fields
from a dorm room in Vermont.
summer,
where has the diaphanous freedom gone?
the smooth skin of moments?

it is not
the grasses that weep.

it is not
the voices of the dead

it is their exhalation—the last breath—that flattens
the tallgrasses that
i saw from the top floor window as they
turned silver as the underside of raspberry leaves, or maple—

the last breath
that weaves across the top of green tongue tips,
a soundless chorus of blades of grass wind made soft like ribbon,
like a finger gracing a cheekbone or
soft flesh-hairline from breasts to bellybutton.

the dead
we are discussing

the dead
their final breath

the dead
exhale a vortex of flutters
around the mouth
hair wisps across the lips
shivers the meadow—
Grass Dancers.

The Blue Curl—when angels fall

We danced on the heads of pins.
—yellow, black, red, or blue—that hold together seams—
what seems to fit into garments
of frayed predicaments with cleverly trimmed cuffs
on sleeves outstretched in prayer for the masses, prayer for nothing,
prayer for everything denied
because suffering is worthy of bloodletting and sleeves
drip not with hearts, but fringe souls
on a twenty-yard skirt—layers of tempestuous ruffles lift
sin-terrifically to midthigh
                spin   spin
blue curl of melodies—soul notes—dangle off the edge that skim
the lizardry our bare feet scrawl in desert sand
this dance of toes that cling to depths of blue

blue night of time-elapsed stars comet 'cross imaginary time zones
celestial tails—brush strokes of spiral—
azure, teal, navy, midnight, turquoise, powder, patina, lapis,
blue, blue, whirring blender blue as the milky way
curls blue as the twisted cedar heartwood blue with fungus,
blue as black eyes, blue as hope stuck
in the throat of fear and fantasy, blue
as the helix bridge of magpies tugging souls
across dinnerware like bi-plane syllabic story banners
talking—a—blue—streak down blue-sky runways talking
with spiders living inside the unused, gun-blue grill—
cigar smoke curls a scent through the lunacy of loneliness
we harbored unsuccessfully in the ceres depths of violence,
into the mulled fragrance of aged rum (which is not blue.)

This is what Sylvie did.
The Sylvie of our aqua fears, our venous self, vascular self.
Sylvie did not dance. That was not her spinning
or painting or running for her life
one hundred-twenty degrees between .50 caliber rounds, dodging, not
       dodging,
death—packed by timeworn stonewalls built by eternity—
desert tan—deaf from blasts, deaf from horror, deaf
from the beaten heart of the universe
that no one dares wander into, across, betwixt
the holy lands of IEDs, boundaries,
perceptions over time squared
divided by unknown x returns.   Time.
             Time of the Serpents and the Shining Ones.
It was not the Sylvie
of our capricious anxiety that tornadoed
between heaven and earth, or torpedo-sliced dark depths
sublime arms retract in sleeves propel as fists—no—no—
not twisted-truth-Sylvie of rage

sequestered in the larynx pressed into glottal stops. No!

                   It was the wind
that strained the fetid smells of summer decomp
through fine wire window screens at two-in-the-morning nightmares—
my eyes hacked open with a disc of full moon.
               And what if it wasn't the moon
                   but a floodlight
            tracking survivors to eliminate?

On the porch, by the grill, right now,
the sun presses my neck like the hands of a lover I have always known.
What   it is   that I was not meant to know?
Not meant to have or hold or love? What is love?
It is taken—always taken—

The Fallen. We have fallen
into lazuli fragments of each betrayal, double-cross,
starving child, dismembered body, and revengeful soul.

The wind in a spinning skirt
sneaks a harmony from thighs to earth
to dust to birth to breasts (atoned for the curves they bring to hands)
that spin the breath, spin the wheel of Kali—Shevic tumblers unlock—
unsheathe the glint of polished steel the tongue tastes
the eyes close to smell the smell of steel and cloves,
mouth waters, drips Larimar onto coral reefs of—
be-gone-stabbing-cobalt-memories-too-sharp-to-paint!
(Why did I think the skirt was a van Gogh abyss of blue?)

In the beginning
we danced atop the heads of pins in the dust
of Temple floors
scrawled the destiny of humans with our stumbling feet
and flying skirts
it was all we knew to know
the whirling in our heads, the rush in our ears, just before
the cold, sweated flesh, heartbeat of flight—
it is all we know
just before the prayers come,
before the promises, the deals, the confessions—
we fall as anyone can fall,
and orbit, suspended

189

waiting for the call
that claims the self that throws to the wind
baubles of trauma and hatred,
angst for the wicked, lust for the bodacious,
bold cacophony of sound, speed of light careening
on the wings of Aquila through the Milky Way
we cast our spectrum and   spin   spin   spin the melodies
              that dance us into the woven cerecloth of duty.

          Drunk on sorrow, our sapphire tears drop,
              we swallow our pride.

Courage Grows Strong at the Wound

A non-forgiving beak—grief.
The stork tore flesh of its chest, vulning, to feed its young.

With this pin of ancestral crest, I draw blood
feeding the next generation is an absolution.

We did not die in vain—"Virescit Vulnere Virtus"
Great wings rise for a down-stroke as a great sword.

I have consumed the flesh of my ancestors who paid it forward
through the triangulation of fate, mission, fool or hero, a fine line

seems to lock into place a reason for living but who's in charge
of striking notes and letters from old scores? Unsettled debts?

Flesh is a lethal substance mapping the future through the past
through the sacrifice of laws, the laws of sacrifice.

No more strategies—no more forthcomings
birds fly with open chests.

The Reincarnation

I walk into the ocean as a Siren's tremolo
teetering on the peaks of Atlantic waves—the froth—
a foam from the gills of creatures, depth and mystery.

I am eaten by stones and whales and wash
in with the tide for little boys and girls to uncover—
morning beaches—seaweed, broken shells, sea-ground glass, treasures.

I let go of anchors and Eagles will claim
what has always belonged to them—their talons
lifting the spirit of diamond silica
from the crests of waves.

I reclaim the water absent at my birth
peel the veil from my infant face
clear the mucous from my angered throat and live
even if it kills me.

This Woman

You are a chert woman.
A sharpened tool.
Paleo edge.
Obsidian edge.

A shearing of viscera
and the womb is gone, the ovaries gone—
Now is the engendered task of burrowing
into the red earth Sahara fog—composed silent caked earth—
dry blood earth fed by the masses—
young girls butchered for the seemingly silent clitoral chip
cracked terra firma groans—haunts this poem
is a war this poem
is political this poem is the violence of my existence and the power
to bleed and to sharpen bones with dancing feet
across the mountainous breasts of all women marching
through the thighs of longing.

I am this chert woman
A tool of power with the shaving edge of silent action.

Fabric

The weaver has become the pattern, plaid
full of angles and predictabilities
and the shuttling of husbands, children, lovers
wears her thin.

There are two movements: past and future.
The loose swatch of the present unravels,
always in ballet fashion,
dangles gracefully between flying and landing.

There is a texture in love that needs to be felt,
needs deft fingers to braid the over-under of self.

Fingers that toe dance over warp and weft,
that understand the rhythm of the loom, the tapestry,
an arabesque of extended tones both subtle and vibrant.

With eyes closed, the clatter of shuttle, and feet pumping the loom
like a grand pipe organ resonating across threads,
she remembers her last words to her first lover,
"like worn denim, love me like that."

About the Author

Ms. Rancourt, Abenaki/Huron descent, is a multi-modal Expressive Arts Therapist with degrees in psychology, and creative writing. Her book of poetry, **Billboard in the Clouds,** received the Native Writers' Circle of the Americas First Book Award. She is a member and guest presenter at the International Expressive Arts Association bi-annual conference 2017/2019, and is an Amherst Writers and Artist Affiliate. Her workshops, artist salons, and readings are known for being authentic, honest, and blessed with humor. Ms. Rancourt's work, regardless of genre, is a connection to nature and the power of place. Inspired by the multiracial poetess, Ai, Ms. Rancourt remarks, "poetry isn't always pastoral fantasy, sometimes it is the skill of finding the beauty in a single moment, a single gesture, and the courage to write about that truth no matter where you are or what is happening around you. Artists have a responsibility."

Ms. Rancourt's work has appeared in *Grey Borders Magazine, Synaeresis: Harmonia Press, Twist in Time, Door Is A Jar, Avatar Review, New Reader Magazine, Tiny Flames Press, Big Pond Rumours, Quiddity, River Heron Review, Shaking the Sheets, The Gyroscope Review, theSame, Young Ravens Literary Review # 8, Tupelo Press Native Voices Anthology, Bright Hill Press 25th Anniversary Anthology, Dawnland Voices 2.0 #4, Northern New England Review, Bear Review, Three Drops Press, mgversion2>datura, Slipstream, Collections of Poetry and Prose, Muddy River Poetry Review, Ginosko, Journal of Military Experience, Cimarron Review, Callaloo.*

Ms. Rancourt is an Aikido and Iaido practitioner and a USMC and Army Veteran who continues to serve as a Mentor for the Saratoga County Veterans' Peer to Peer program. You can reach Ms. Rancourt for readings, Artist Salons, workshops and more via her website: www.expressive-arts.com

About the Cover Artist

Tif Holmes is a photographic artist with a unique background of more than twenty-five years in the performing arts as musician and educator, eight years in the United States Army, and ten plus years behind a camera. Her images have been featured in exhibitions and publications in the United States, abroad, and featured on/in multiple magazines and books. She is founder and director of Engage the Light, a community organization for veterans, and at-risk communities, who use expressive photography to engage one another and their world with compassion and creativity. Tif works extensively with the veteran community. She is regularly invited to speak at events hosted by organizations for women, veterans, and healthcare professionals about the effectiveness of expressive photography as a tool for communication and healing. Tif is a highly sought-after portrait photographer for creative artists. She is an avid backpacker, wilderness guru, dog lover, and eternally enthusiastic explorer of wild places. For more information visit www.tifholmes.com.

About the Press

Unsolicited Press was founded in 2012 and is based in Portland, Oregon. The small press produces works of fiction, poetry, and creative nonfiction written by award-winning authors.

Learn more at www.unsolicitedpress.com.

Acknowledgements

"The Smell of Blood," "Maccha "appearing as Matcha in *murmurs at the gate* , and "Fabric," forthcoming https://www.tupelopress.org/product/native-voices-indigenous-american-poetry-craft-and-conversations/

"Courage Grows Strong at the Wound," and "Steelies" **Like Light: 25th Anniversary Anthology,** Bertha Rogers, Editor

"Serf" www.snapdragonjournal.com

"Impressive Education," "Maccha," "Mediterranean Blues," and "When the Glacier is Gone." Dawnland Voices 2.0 # 4, May 2017.

"Mish'ala," "Caput Mortuum," "Curves of Grace," mgversion2>datura #87
"Reenlistment," "The Execution," "The Golden Hour," "Ba Boom," "When We Were Close," "on my way home." Collections of Poetry and Prose Editor: Robin Barratt, UK.

"When the Wind Stops," "Ghost Nets" Ginosko Anthology #3, Mad Hat Press 2017.

"The Darkest Spot is Light" Slipstream Issue #36, 2016.

"The Fabric," "So Many Selves," "My Lidocaine Love," "The Reticent Veil" in **The American Institute of Stress quarterly Combat Stress** magazine, Feb, 2016. http://www.stress.org/wp-content/uploads/Newsletter/January_2016_Combat_Stress/index.html?utm_source=January+2016+Combat+Stress&utm_campaign=January+2016+Combat+Stress&utm_medium=email

"Venom, Sweet Venom," "A Bridge of Social Renaissance" "the dead are not dead" **In the Trenches Anthology**, Krista Clark Grabowski, Verto Publishing.

"Harvesting the Spring" Four Winds Literary Magazine, Vol. II.

"The Baby Singer" Chiron Review, #98.

"The Smell of Blood", "Why I don't Meditate" Blue Streak Journal of Military Poetry.
"The Hunt", "Ghost Nets", "Tsunami Conflict", "Visions of Clara", "Throwing Stars" The Journal of Military Experience, vol. II.

"The Reticent Veil" Veterans Writing Project, O Dark Thirty—Rear Support.

"Sons and Fathers" Muddy River Poetry Review.

"Fanning Fire" "Singing Across the River," Angie's Diary, 27Sept2011, 4Oct2011.

"Fanning Fire", "Singing Across the River", Saranac Review, 2nd Edition.

"When the Wind Stops", "Ghost Nets", "Not Tonight", "The Edge" Ginosko 11.

"The Negative" "The Viewing" Letters to Fathers from Daughters.

"The Reticent Veil", "The Edge" "Sons and Fathers" translated into French by Beatrice Machet-Franke. http://amb.boudet.perso.sfr.fr/surledos12.htm

"Singing Across the River" Dawnland Voices—An Anthology of Indigenous Writing from New England. Univ. of Nebraska Press.

"Between Lovers and Light" Cimarron Review #121.

"The Silver Side" The Albany Review.

"Harvesting the Spring" The Rooster Bay Poetry Review.

"There Are No Wrong Numbers" (Published under Suzanne S. Pierce.) American Poetry Anthology, Vol. IX, Number 1.

"Crooked Nose," "Throwing Stars," and "The Viewing" first appeared in The

CPSIA information can be obtained
at www.ICGtesting.com
Printed in the USA
LVHW091755091019
633689LV00004B/740/P